Twenty-Five Villag

Charles Kingsley

Alpha Editions

This edition published in 2024

ISBN : 9789362516428

Design and Setting By
Alpha Editions
www.alphaedis.com
Email - info@alphaedis.com

As per information held with us this book is in Public Domain.
This book is a reproduction of an important historical work. Alpha Editions uses the best technology to reproduce historical work in the same manner it was first published to preserve its original nature. Any marks or number seen are left intentionally to preserve its true form.

Contents

SERMON I. GOD'S WORLD. .... - 1 -
SERMON II. RELIGION NOT GODLINESS. .... - 7 -
SERMON III. LIFE AND DEATH. .... - 13 -
SERMON IV. THE WORK OF GOD'S SPIRIT. .... - 18 -
SERMON V. FAITH. .... - 24 -
SERMON VI. THE SPIRIT AND THE FLESH. .... - 30 -
SERMON VII. RETRIBUTION. .... - 36 -
SERMON VIII. SELF-DESTRUCTION. .... - 41 -
SERMON IX. HELL ON EARTH. .... - 45 -
SERMON X. NOAH'S JUSTICE. .... - 51 -
SERMON XI. THE NOACHIC COVENANT. .... - 56 -
SERMON XII. ABRAHAM'S FAITH. .... - 61 -
SERMON XIII. ABRAHAM'S OBEDIENCE. .... - 68 -
SERMON XIV. OUR FATHER IN HEAVEN. .... - 73 -
SERMON XV. THE TRANSFIGURATION. .... - 78 -
SERMON XVI. THE CRUCIFIXION. .... - 84 -
SERMON XVII. THE RESURRECTION. .... - 87 -
SERMON XVIII. IMPROVEMENT. .... - 93 -
SERMON XIX. MAN'S WORKING DAY. .... - 97 -
SERMON XX. ASSOCIATION. .... - 102 -
SERMON XXI. HEAVEN ON EARTH. .... - 106 -
SERMON XXII. NATIONAL PRIVILEGES. .... - 110 -
SERMON XXIII. LENTEN THOUGHTS. .... - 115 -
SERMON XXIV. ON BOOKS. .... - 120 -
SERMON XXV. THE COURAGE OF THE SAVIOUR. ... - 125 -
FOOTNOTES .... - 130 -

SERMON I.
GOD'S WORLD.

Psalm civ. 24.

"O Lord, how manifold are Thy works! in wisdom hast Thou made them all: the earth is full of Thy riches."

When we read such psalms as the one from which this verse is taken, we cannot help, if we consider, feeling at once a great difference between them and any hymns or religious poetry which is commonly written or read in these days. The hymns which are most liked now, and the psalms which people most willingly choose out of the Bible, are those which speak, or seem to speak, about God's dealings with people's own souls, while such psalms as this are overlooked. People do not care really about psalms of this kind when they find them in the Bible, and they do not expect or wish nowadays any one to write poetry like them. For these psalms of which I speak praise and honour God, not for what He has done to our souls, but for what He has done and is doing in the world around us. This very 104th psalm, for instance, speaks entirely about things which we hardly care or even think proper to mention in church now. It speaks of this earth entirely, and the things on it. Of the light, the clouds, and wind—of hills and valleys, and the springs on the hill-sides—of wild beasts and birds—of grass and corn, and wine and oil—of the sun and moon, night and day—the great sea, the ships, and the fishes, and all the wonderful and nameless creatures which people the waters—the very birds' nests in the high trees, and the rabbits burrowing among the rocks,—nothing on the earth but this psalm thinks it worth mentioning. And all this, which one would expect to find only in a book of natural history, is in the Bible, in one of the psalms, written to be sung in the temple at Jerusalem, before the throne of the living God and His glory which used to be seen in that temple,—inspired, as we all believe, by God's Spirit,—God's own word, in short: that is worth thinking of. Surely the man who wrote this must have thought very differently about this world, with its fields and woods, and beasts and birds, from what we think. Suppose, now, that we had been old Jews in the temple, standing before the holy house, and that we believed, as the Jews believed, that there was only one thin wall and one curtain of linen between us and the glory of the living God, that unspeakable brightness and majesty which no one could look at for fear of instant death, except the high-priest in fear and trembling once a-year—that inside that small holy house, He, God Almighty, appeared visibly—God who made heaven and earth. Suppose we had been there in the temple, and known all this, should we have liked to be singing about beasts and birds, with God Himself close to us? We should not have liked it—we should have been terrified, thinking perhaps about our own sinfulness, perhaps about that wonderful majesty which dwelt inside. We should have wished to say or sing something spiritual, as we call it; at all events, something very different from the 104th psalm about woods, and rivers, and dumb beasts. We do not like the thought of such a thing: it seems almost irreverent, almost impertinent to God to be talking of such things in His presence. Now does this shew us that we think about this earth, and the things in it, in a very different way from those old Jews? They thought it a fit and proper thing to talk about corn and wine and oil, and cattle and fishes, in the presence of Almighty God, and we do not think it fit and proper. We read this psalm when it comes in the Church-service as a matter of course, mainly because we do not believe that God is here among us. We should not be so ready to read it if we thought that Almighty God was so near us.

That is a great difference between us and the old Jews. Whether it shews that we are better or not than they were in the main, I cannot tell; perhaps some of them had such thoughts too, and said, 'It is not respectful to God to talk about such commonplace earthly things in His presence;' perhaps some of them thought themselves spiritual and pure-minded for looking down on this psalm, and on David for writing it. Very likely, for men have had such thoughts in all ages, and will have them. But the man who wrote this psalm had no such thoughts. He said himself, in this same psalm, that his words would please God. Nay, he is not speaking and preaching *about* God in this psalm, as I am now in my sermon, but he is doing more; he is speaking *to* God—a much more solemn thing if you will think of it. He says, "O Lord my God, *Thou* art become exceeding glorious. Thou deckest Thyself with light as with a garment. All the beasts wait on Thee; when Thou givest them meat they gather it. Thou renewest the face of the earth." When he turns and speaks of God as "He," saying, "He appointed the moon," and so on, he cannot help going back to God, and pouring out his wonder, and delight, and awe, to God Himself, as we would sooner speak *to* any one we love and honour than merely speak *about* them. He cannot take his mind off God. And just at the last, when he does turn and speak to himself, it is to say, "Praise thou the Lord, O my soul, praise the Lord," as if rebuking and stirring up himself for being too cold-hearted and slow, for not admiring and honouring enough the infinite wisdom, and power, and love, and glorious majesty of God, which to him shines out in every hedge-side bird and every blade of grass. Truly I said that man had a very different way of looking at God's earth from what we have!

Now, in what did that difference lie? What was it? We need not look far to see. It was this,—David looked on the earth as God's earth; we look on it as man's earth, or nobody's earth. We know that we are here, with trees and grass, and beasts and birds, round us. And we know that we did not put them here; and that, after we are dead and gone, they will go on just as they went on before we were born,—each tree, and flower, and animal, after its kind, but we know nothing more. The earth is here, and we on it; but who put it there, and why it is there, and why we are on it, instead of being anywhere else, few ever think. But to David the earth looked very different; it had quite another meaning; it spoke to him of God who made it. By seeing what this earth is like, he saw what God who made it is like: and we see no such thing. The earth?—we can eat the corn and cattle on it, we can earn money by farming it, and ploughing and digging it; and that is all most men know about it. But David knew something more—something which made him feel himself very weak, and yet very safe; very ignorant and stupid, and yet honoured with glorious knowledge from God,—something which made him feel that he belonged to this world, and must not forget it or neglect it, that this earth was his lesson-book—this earth was his work-field; and yet those same thoughts which shewed him how he was made for the land round him, and the land round him was made for him, shewed him also that he belonged to another world—a spirit-world; shewed him that when this world passed away, he should live for ever; shewed him that while he had a mortal body, he had an immortal soul too; shewed him that though his home and business were here on earth, yet that, for that very reason, his home and business were in heaven, with God who made the earth, with that blessed One of whom he said, "Thou, Lord, in the beginning hast laid the foundation of the earth, and the heavens are the work of thy hands. They shall perish, but Thou shalt endure; they all shall fade as a garment, and like a vesture shalt Thou change them, and they shall be changed; but Thou art the same, and *Thy* years shall not fail. The children of Thy servants shall continue, and their seed shall stand fast in Thy sight." "As a garment shalt Thou change them,"—ay, there was David's secret! He saw that this earth and skies are God's garment—the garment by which we see God; and that is what our forefathers saw too, and just what we have forgotten; but David had not forgotten it. Look at this very 104th psalm again, how he refers every thing to God. We say, 'The light shines:' David says something more; he says, "Thou, O God, adornest Thyself with light as with a curtain." Light is a picture of God. "God," says St. John, "is light, and in Him is no darkness at all." We say, 'The clouds fly and the wind blows,' as if they went of themselves; David says, "God makes the clouds His chariot, and walks upon the wings of the wind." We talk of the rich airs of spring, of the flashing lightning of summer, as dead things; and men who call themselves wise say, that lightning is only matter,—'We can grind the like of it out of glass and silk, and make lightning for ourselves in a small way;' and so they can in a small way, and in a very small one: David does not deny that, but he puts us in mind of something in that lightning and those breezes which we cannot make. He says, God makes the winds His angels, and flaming fire his ministers; and St. Paul takes the same text, and turns it round to suit his purpose, when he is talking of the blessed angels, saying, 'That text in the 104th Psalm means something more; it means that God makes His angels spirits, (that is winds) and His ministers a flaming fire.' So shewing us that in those breezes there are living spirits, that God's angels guide those thunder-clouds; that the roaring thunderclap is a shock in the air truly, but that it is something more—that it is the voice of God, which shakes the cedar-trees of Lebanon, and tears down the thick bushes, and makes the wild deer slip their young. So we read in the psalms in church; that is David's account of the thunder. I take it for a true account; you may or not as you like. See again. Those springs in the hill-sides, how do they come there? 'Rain-water soaking and flowing out,' we say. True, but David says something more; he says, God sends the springs, and He sends them into the rivers too. You may say, 'Why, water must run down-hill, what need of God?' But suppose God had chosen that water should run *up*-hill and not down, how would it have been then?—Very different, I think. No; He sends them; He sends all things. Wherever there is any thing useful, His Spirit has settled it. The help that is done on earth He doeth it all Himself.—Loving and merciful,—caring for the poor dumb beasts!—He sends the springs, and David says, "All the beasts of the field drink thereof." The wild animals in the night, He cares for them too,—He, the Almighty God. We hear the foxes bark by night, and we think the fox is hungry, and there it ends with us; but not with David: he says, "The lions roaring after their prey do seek their meat from God,"—God, who feedeth the young ravens who call upon Him. He is a God! "He did not make the world," says a wise man, "and then let it spin round His finger," as we wind up a watch, and then leave it to go of itself. No; "His mercy is over all His works." Loving and merciful, the God of nature is the God of grace. The same love which chose us and our forefathers for His people while we were yet dead in trespasses and sins; the same only-begotten Son, who came down on earth to die for us poor wretches on the cross,—that same love, that same power, that same Word of God, who made heaven and earth, looks after the poor gnats in the winter time, that they may have a chance of coming out of the ground when the day stirs the little life in them, and dance in the sunbeam for a short hour of gay life, before they return to the dust whence they were made, to feed creatures nobler and more precious than themselves. That is all God's doing, all the doing of Christ, the King of the earth. "They wait on Him," says David. The beasts, and birds, and insects, the strange fish, and shells, and the nameless corals too, in the deep, deep sea, who build and build below the water for years and thousands of years, every little, tiny creature bringing his atom of lime to add to the great heap, till their heap stands out of the water and becomes dry land; and seeds float thither over the wide waste sea, and trees grow up, and birds are driven thither by storms; and men come by accident in stray ships, and build, and sow, and multiply, and raise churches, and worship the God of heaven, and Christ, the blessed One,—on that new land which the little coral worms have built up from the deep. Consider that. Who sent them there? Who contrived that those particular men should light on that new island at that especial time? Who guided thither those seeds—those birds? Who gave those insects that strange longing and power to build and build on continually?—Christ, by whom all things are made, to whom all power is given in heaven and earth; He and His Spirit, and none else. It is when *He* opens His hand, they are filled with good. It is when *He* takes away their breath, they die, and turn again to their dust. *He* lets His breath, His spirit, go forth, and out of that dead dust grow plants and herbs afresh for man and beast, and He renews the face of the earth. For, says the wise man, "all things are God's garment"—outward and visible signs of His unseen and unapproachable glory; and when they are worn out, He changes them, says the Psalmist, as a garment, and they shall be changed.

The old order changes, giving place to the new,
And God fulfils Himself in many ways.

But He is the same. He is there all the time. All things are His work. In all things we may see Him, if our souls have eyes. All things, be they what they may, which live and grow on this earth, or happen on land or in the sky, will tell us a tale of God,—shew forth some one feature, at least, of our blessed Saviour's countenance and character,—either His foresight, or His wisdom, or His order, or His power, or His love, or His condescension, or His long-suffering, or His slow, sure vengeance on those who break His laws. It is all written there outside in the great green book, which God has given to labouring men, and which neither taxes nor tyrants can take from them. The man who is no scholar in letters may read of God as he follows the plough, for the earth he ploughs is his Father's: there is God's mark and seal on it,—His name, which though it is written on the dust, yet neither man nor fiend can wipe it out!

The poor, solitary, untaught boy, who keeps the sheep, or minds the birds, long lonely days, far from his mother and his playmates, may keep alive in him all purifying thoughts, if he will but open his eyes and look at the green earth around him.

Think now, my boys, when you are at your work, how all things may put you in mind of God, if you do but choose. The trees which shelter you from the wind, God planted them there for your sakes, in His love.—There is a lesson about God. The birds which you drive off the corn, who gave them the sense to keep together and profit by each other's wit and keen eyesight? Who but God, who feeds the young birds when they call on Him?—There is another lesson about God. The sheep whom you follow, who ordered the warm wool to grow on them, from which your clothes are made? Who but the Spirit of God above, who clothes the grass of the field, the silly sheep, and who clothes you, too, and thinks of you when you don't think of yourselves?—There is another lesson about God. The feeble lambs in spring, they ought to remind you surely of your blessed Saviour, the Lamb of God, who died for you upon the cruel cross, who was led as a lamb to the slaughter; and like a sheep that lies dumb and patient under the shearer's hand, so he opened not his mouth. Are not these lambs, then, a lesson from God? And these are but one or two examples out of thousands and thousands. Oh, that I could make you, young and old, all feel these things! Oh, that I could make you see God in every thing, and every thing in God! Oh, that I could make you look on this earth, not as a mere dull, dreary prison, and workhouse for your mortal bodies, but as a living book, to speak to you at every time of the living God, Father, Son, and Holy Ghost! Sure I am that that would be a heavenly life for you,—sure I am that it would keep you from many a sin, and stir you up to many a holy thought and deed, if you could learn to find in every thing around you, however small or mean, the work of God's hand, the likeness of God's countenance, the shadow of God's glory.

SERMON II.
RELIGION NOT GODLINESS.

Psalm civ. 13–15.

"He watereth the hills from his chambers: the earth is satisfied with the fruit of thy works. He causeth the grass to grow for the cattle, and herb for the service of man: that he may bring forth food out of the earth; and wine that maketh glad the heart of man, and oil to make his face to shine, and bread which strengtheneth man's heart."

Did you ever remark, my friends, that the Bible says hardly any thing about religion—that it never praises religious people? This is very curious. Would to God we would all remember it! The Bible speaks of a religious man only once, and of religion only twice, except where it speaks of the Jews' religion to condemn it, and shews what an empty, blind, useless thing it was.

What does this Bible talk of, then? It talks of God; not of religion, but of God. It tells us not to be religious, but to be godly. You may think there is no difference, or that it is but a difference of words. I tell you that a difference in words is a very awful, important difference. A difference in words is a difference in things. Words are very awful and wonderful things, for they come from the most awful and wonderful of all beings, Jesus Christ, the Word. He puts words into men's minds—He made all things, and He makes all words to express those things with. And woe to those who use the wrong words about things!—For if a man calls any thing by its wrong name, it is a sure sign that he understands that thing wrongly, or feels about it wrongly; and therefore a man's words are oftener honester than he thinks; for as a man's words are, so is a man's heart; out of the abundance of our hearts our mouths speak; and, therefore, by right words, by the right names which we call things, we shall be justified, and by our words, by the wrong names we call things, we shall be condemned.

Therefore a difference in words is a difference in the things which those words mean, and there is a difference between religion and godliness; and we shew it by our words. Now these are religious times, but they are very ungodly times; and we shew that also by our words. Because we think that people ought to be religious, we talk a great deal about religion; because we hardly think at all that a man ought to be godly, we talk very little about God, and that good old Bible word "godliness" does not pass our lips once a-month. For a man may be very religious, my friends, and yet very ungodly. The heathens were very religious at the very time that, as St. Paul tells us, they would not keep God in their knowledge. The Jews were the most religious people on the earth, they hardly talked or thought about anything but religion, at the very time that they knew so little of God that they crucified Him when He came down among them. St. Paul says that he was living after the strictest sect of the Jews' religion, at the very time that he was fighting against God, persecuting God's people and God's Son, and dead in trespasses and sins. These are ugly facts, my friends, but they are true, and well worth our laying to heart in these religious, ungodly days. I am afraid if Jesus Christ came down into England this day as a carpenter's son, He would get—a better hearing, perhaps, than the Jews gave him, but still a very bad hearing—one dare hardly think of it.

And yet I believe we ought to think of it, and, by God's help, I will one day preach you a sermon, asking you all round this fair question:—If Jesus Christ came to you in the shape of a poor man, whom nobody knew, should *you* know him? should you admire him, fall at his feet and give yourself up to him body and soul? I am afraid that I, for one, should not—I am afraid that too many of us here would not. That comes of thinking more of religion than we do of godliness—in plain words, more of our own souls than we do of Jesus Christ. But you will want to know what is, after all, the difference between religion and godliness? Just the difference, my friends, that there is between always thinking of self and always forgetting self—between the terror of a slave and the affection of a child—between the fear of hell and the love of God. For, tell me, what you mean by being religious? Do you not mean thinking a great deal about your own souls, and praying and reading about your own souls, and trying by all possible means to get your own souls saved? Is not that the meaning of religion? And yet I have never mentioned God's name in describing it! This sort of religion must have very little to do with God. You may be surprised at my words, and say in your hearts almost angrily, 'Why who saves our souls but God? therefore religion must have to do with God.' But, my friends, for your souls' sake, and for God's sake, ask yourselves this question on your knees this day:—If you could get your souls saved without God's help, would it make much difference to you? Suppose an angel from heaven, as they say, was to come down and prove to you clearly that there was no God, no blessed Jesus in heaven, that the world made itself, and went on of itself, and that the Bible was all a mistake, but that you need not mind, for your gardens and crops would grow just as well, and your souls be saved just as well when you died.

To how many of you would it make any difference? To some of you, thank God, I believe it would make a difference. Here are some here, I believe, who would feel that news the worst news they ever heard,—worse than if they were told that their souls were lost for ever; there are some here, I do believe, who, at that news, would cry aloud in agony, like little children who had lost their father, and say, 'No Father in heaven to love? No blessed Jesus in heaven to work for, and die for, and glory and delight in? No God to rule and manage this poor, miserable, quarrelsome world, bringing good out of evil, blessing and guiding all things and people on earth? What do I care what becomes of my soul if there is no God for my soul to glory in? What is heaven worth without God? God is Heaven!'

Yes, indeed, what would heaven be worth without God? But how many people feel that the curse of this day is, that most people have forgotten *that*? They are selfishly anxious enough about their own souls, but they have forgotten God. They are religious, for fear of hell; but they are not godly, for they do not love God, or see God's hand in every thing. They forget that they have a Father in heaven; that He sends rain, and sunshine, and fruitful seasons; that He gives them all things richly to enjoy in spite of all their sins. His mercies are far above, out of their sight, and therefore His judgments are far away out of their sight too; and so they talk of the "Visitation of God," as if it was something that was very extraordinary, and happened very seldom; and when it came, only brought evil, harm, and sorrow. If a man lives on in health, they say he lives by the strength of his own constitution; if he drops down dead, they say he died by "the visitation of God." If the corn-crops go on all right and safe, they think *that* quite natural—the effect of the soil, and the weather, and their own skill in farming and gardening. But if there comes a hailstorm or a blight, and spoils it all, and brings on a famine, they call it at once "a visitation of God." My friends! do you think God "visits" the earth or you only to harm you? I tell you that every blade of grass grows by "the visitation of God." I tell you that every healthy breath you ever drew, every cheerful hour you ever spent, every good crop you ever housed safely, came to you by "the visitation of God." I tell you that every sensible thought or plan that ever came into your heads,—every loving, honest, manly, womanly feeling that ever rose in your hearts, God "visited" you to put it there. If God's Spirit had not given it you, you would never have got it of yourselves.

But people forget this, and therefore they have so little real love to God—so little real, loyal, childlike trust in God. They do not think much about God, because they find no pleasure in thinking about Him; they look on God as a task-master, gathering where He has not strewed, reaping where He has not sown,—a task-master who has put them, very miserable, sinful creatures, to struggle on in a very miserable, sinful world, and, though He tells them in His Bible that they *cannot* keep His commandments, expects them to keep them just the same, and will at the last send them all into everlasting fire, unless they take a great deal of care, and give up a great many natural and pleasant things, and beseech and entreat Him very hard to excuse them, after all. This is the thought which most people have of God, even religious people; they look on God as a stern tyrant, who, when man sinned and fell, could not satisfy His own justice—His own vengeance in plain words, without killing some one, and who would have certainly killed all mankind, if Jesus Christ had not interfered, and said, "If Thou must slay some one, slay me, though I am innocent!"

Oh, my friends, does not this all sound horrible and irreverent? And yet if you will but look into your own hearts, will you not find some such thoughts there? I am sure you will. I believe every man finds such thoughts in his heart now and then. I find them in my own heart: I know that they must be in the hearts of others, because I see them producing their natural fruits in people's actions—a selfish, slavish view of religion, with little or no real love to God, or real trust in Him; but a great deal of uneasy dread of Him: for this is just the dark, false view of God, and of the good news of salvation and the kingdom of heaven, which the devil is always trying to make men take. The Evil One tries to make us forget that God is love; he tries to make us forget that God gives us all things richly to enjoy; he tries to make us forget that God gives at all, and to make us think that we take, not that He gives; to make us look at God as a task-master, not as a father; in one word, to make us mistake the devil for God, and God for the devil.

And, therefore, it is that we ought to bless God for such Scriptures as this 104th Psalm, which He seems to have preserved in the Bible just to contradict these dark, slavish notions,—just to testify that God is a *giver*, and knows our necessities before we ask and gives us all things, even as He gave us His Blessed Son—freely, long before we wanted them,—from the foundation of all things, before ever the earth and the world was made—from all eternity, perpetual love, perpetual bounty.

What does this text teach us? To look at God as Him who gives to all freely and upbraideth not. It says to us,—Do not suppose that your crops grow of themselves. God waters the hills from above. He causes the grass to grow for the cattle, and the green herb for the service of man. Do not suppose that He cares nothing about seeing you comfortable and happy. It is He, He only who sends all which strengthens man's body, and makes glad his heart, and makes him of a cheerful countenance. His will is that you should be cheerful. Ah, my friends, if we would but believe all this!—we are too apt to say to ourselves, 'Our earthly comforts here have nothing to do with godliness or God, God must save our souls, but our bodies we must save ourselves. God gives us spiritual blessings, but earthly blessings, the good things of this life, for them we must scramble and drudge ourselves, and get as much of them as we can without offending God;'—as if God grudged us our comforts! as if godliness had not the promise of this life as well as the life to come! If we would but believe that God knows our necessities before we ask—that He gives us daily more than we can ever get by working for it!—if we would but seek first the kingdom of God and His righteousness, all other things would be added to us; and we should find that he who loses his life should save it. And this way of looking at God's earth would not make us idle; it would not tempt us to sit with folded hands for God's blessings to drop into our mouths. No! I believe it would make men far more industrious than ever mere self-interest can make them; they would say, 'God is our Father, He gave us His own Son, He gives us all things freely, we owe Him not slavish service, but a boundless debt of cheerful gratitude. Therefore we must do His will, and we are sure His will must be our happiness and comfort—therefore we must do His will, and His will is that we should *work*, and therefore we *must* work. He has bidden us labour on this earth—He has bidden us dress it and keep it, conquer it and fill it for Him. We are His stewards here on earth, and therefore it is a glory and an honour to be allowed to work here in God's own land—in our loving Father's own garden. We do not know why He wishes us to labour and till the ground, for He could have fed us with manna from heaven if He liked, as He fed the Jews of old, without our working at all. But His will is that we should work; and work we will, not for our own sakes merely, but for His sake, because we know He likes it, and for the sake of our brothers, our countrymen, for whom Christ died.'

Oh, my friends, why is it that so many till the ground industriously, and yet grow poorer and poorer for all their drudging and working? It is their own fault. They till the ground for their own sakes, and not for God's sake and for their countrymen's sake; and so, as the Prophet says, they sow much and bring in little, and he who earns wages earns them to put in a bag full of holes. Suppose you try the opposite plan. Suppose you say to yourself, 'I will work henceforward because God wishes me to work. I will work henceforward for my country's sake, because I feel that God has given me a noble and a holy calling when He set me to grow food for His children, the people of England. As for my wages and my profit, God will take care of them if they are just; and if they are unjust, He will take care of them too. He, at all events, makes the garden and the field grow, and not I. My land is filled, not with the fruit of my work, but with the fruit of His work. He will see that I lose nothing by my labour. If I till the soil for God and for God's children, I may trust God to pay me my wages.' Oh, my friends, He who feeds the young birds when they call upon Him; and far, far more, He who gave you His only-begotten Son, will He not with Him freely give you all things? For, after all done, He must give to you, or you will not get. You may fret and stint, and scrape and puzzle; one man may sow, and another man may water; but, after all, who can give the increase but God? Can you make a load of hay, unless He has first grown it for you, and then dried it for you? If you would but think a little more about Him, if you would believe that your crops were His gifts, and in your hearts offer them up to Him as thank-offerings, see if He would not help you to sell your crops as well as to house them. He would put you in the way of an honest profit for your labour, just as surely as He only put you in the way of labouring at all. "Trust in the Lord, and be doing good; dwell in the land, and verily thou shalt be fed;" for "without me," says our Lord, "you can do nothing." No: these are His own words—nothing. To Him all power is given in heaven and earth; He knows every root and every leaf, and feeds it. Will He not much more feed you, oh ye of little faith? Do you think that He has made His world so ill that a man cannot get on in it unless he is a rogue? No. Cast all your care on Him, and see if you do not find out ere long that He cares for you, and has cared for you from all eternity.

SERMON III.
LIFE AND DEATH.

Psalm civ. 24, 28–30.

"O Lord, how manifold are Thy works! in wisdom hast Thou made them all: the earth is full of Thy riches. That Thou givest them they gather: Thou openest Thine hand, they are filled with good. Thou hidest Thy face, they are troubled: Thou takest away their breath, they die, and return to their dust. Thou sendest forth Thy spirit, they are created: and Thou renewest the face of the earth."

I HAD intended to go through this psalm with you in regular order; but things have happened this parish, awful and sad, during the last week, which I was bound not to let slip without trying to bring them home to your hearts, if by any means I could persuade the thoughtless ones among you to be wise and consider your latter end:—I mean the sad deaths of various of our acquaintances. The death-bell has been tolled in this parish three times, I believe, in one day—a thing which has seldom happened before, and which God grant may never happen again. Within two miles of this church there are now five lying dead. Five human beings, young as well as old, to whom the awful words of the text have been fulfilled: "Thou takest away their breath, they die, and return to their dust." And the very day on which three of these deaths happened was Ascension-day—the day on which Jesus, the Lord of life, the Conqueror of death, ascended upon high, having led captivity captive, and became the first-fruits of the grave, to send down from the heaven of eternal life the Spirit who is the Giver of life. That was a strange mixture, death seemingly triumphant over Christ's people on the very day on which life triumphed in Jesus Christ Himself. Let us see, though, whether death has not something to do with Ascension-day. Let us see whether a sermon about death is not a fit sermon for the Sunday after Ascension-day. Let us see whether the text has not a message about life and death too—a message which may make us feel that in the midst of life we are in death, and that yet in the midst of death we are in life; that however things may *seem*, yet death has not conquered life, but life has conquered and *will* conquer death, and conquer it most completely at the very moment that we die, and our bodies return to their dust.

Do I speak riddles? I think the text will explain my riddles, for it tells us how life comes, how death comes. Life comes from God: He sends forth His spirit, and things are made, and He renews the face of the earth. We read in the very two verses of the book of Genesis how the Spirit of God moved upon the face of the waters the creation, and woke all things into life. Therefore the Creed well calls the Holy Ghost, the Spirit of God, that is—the Lord and Giver of life. And the text tells us that He gives life, not only to us who have immortal souls, but to every thing on the face of the earth; for the psalm has been talking all through, not only of men, but of beasts, fishes, trees, and rivers, and rocks, sun and moon. Now, all these things have a life in them. Not a life like ours; but still you speak rightly and wisely when you say, 'That tree is alive, and, That tree is dead. That running water is live water—it is sweet and fresh, but if it is kept standing it begins to putrefy, its life is gone from it, and a sort of death comes over it, and makes it foul, and unwholesome, and unfit to drink.' This is a deep matter, this, how there is a sort of life in every thing, even to the stones under our feet. I do not mean, of course, that stones can think as our life makes us do, or feel as the beasts' life makes them do, or even grow as the trees' life makes them do; but I mean that their life keeps them as they are, without changing or decaying. You hear miners and quarrymen talk very truly of the live rock. That stone, they say, was cut out of the live rock, meaning the rock as it is under ground, sound and hard—as it would be, for aught we know, to the end of time, unless it was taken out of the ground, out of the place where God's Spirit meant it to be, and brought up to the open air and the rain, in which it is not its nature to be. And then you will see that the life of the stone begins to pass from it bit by bit, that it crumbles and peels away, and, in short, decays and is turned again to its dust. Its organisation, as it is called, or life, ends, and then—what? does the stone lie for ever useless? No! And there is the great blessed mystery of how God's Spirit is always bringing life out of death. When the stone is decayed and crumbled down to dust and clay, it makes *soil*—this very soil here, which you plough, is the decayed ruins of ancient hills; the clay which you dig up in the fields was once part of some slate or granite mountains, which were worn away by weather and water, that they might become fruitful earth. Wonderful! but any one who has studied these things can tell you they are true. Any one who has ever lived in mountainous countries ought to have seen the thing happen, ought to know that the land in the mountain valleys is made at first, and kept rich year by year, by the washings from the hills above; and this is the reason why land left dry by rivers and by the sea is generally so rich. Then what becomes of the soil? It begins a new life. The roots of the plants take it up; the salts which they find in it—the staple, as we call them—go to make leaves and seed; the very sand has its use, it feeds the stalks of corn and grass, and makes them stiff. The corn-stalks would never stand upright if they could not get sand from the soil. So what a thousand years ago made part of a mountain, now makes part of a wheat-plant; and in a year more the wheat grain will have been eaten, and the wheat straw perhaps eaten too, and they will have *died*—decayed in the bodies of the animals who have eaten them, and then they will begin a third new life—they will be turned into parts of the animal's body—of a man's body. So that what is now your bone and flesh, may have been once a rock on some hillside a hundred miles away.

Strange, but true! all learned men know that it is true. You, if you think over my words, may see that they are at least reasonable. But still most wonderful! This world works right well, surely. It obeys God's Spirit. Oh, my friends, if we fulfilled our life and our duty as well as the clay which we tread on does,—if we obeyed God's Spirit as surely as the flint does, we should have many a heartache spared us, and many a headache too! To be what God wants us!—to be *men*, to be *women*, and therefore to live as children of God, members of Christ, fulfilling our duty in that state to which God has called us, that would be our bliss and glory. Nothing can live in a state in which God did not intend it to live. Suppose a tree could move itself about like an animal, and chose to do so, the tree would wither and die; it would be trying to act contrary to the law which God has given it. Suppose the ox chose to eat meat like the lion, it would fall sick and die; for it would be acting contrary to the law which God's Spirit had made for it—going out of the calling to which God's Word has called it, to eat grass and not flesh, and live thereby. And so with us: if we will do wickedly, when the will of God, as the Scripture tells us, is our sanctification, our holiness; if we will speak lies, when God's law for us is that we should speak truth; if we will bear hatred and ill-will, when God's law for us is, Love as brothers,—you all sprang from one father, Adam,—you were all redeemed by one brother, Jesus Christ; if we will try to live as if there was no God, when God's law for us is, that a man can live like a man only by faith and trust in God;—then we shall *die*, if we break God's laws according to which he intended man to live. Thus it was with Adam; God intended him to obey God, to learn every thing from God. He chose to disobey God, to try and know something of himself, by getting the knowledge of good and evil; and so death passed on him. He became an unnatural man, a *bad* man, more or less, and so he became a dead man; and death came into the world, that time at least, by sin, by breaking the law by which man was meant to be a man. As the beasts will die if you give them unnatural food, or in any way prevent their following the laws which God has made for them, so man dies, of necessity. All the world cannot help his dying, because he breaks the laws which God has made for him.

And how does he die? The text tells us, God takes away his breath, and turns His face from him. In His presence, it is written, is life. The moment He withdraws his Spirit, the Spirit of life, from any thing, body or soul, then it dies. It was by *sin* came death—by man's becoming unfit for the Spirit of God.

Therefore the body is dead because of sin, says St. Paul, doomed to die, carrying about in it the seeds of death from the very moment it is born. Death has truly passed upon all men!

Most sad; and yet there is hope, and more than hope, there is certain assurance, for us, that though we die, yet shall we live! I have shewn you, in the beginning of my sermon, how nothing that dies perishes to nothing, but begins a new and a higher life. How the stone becomes a plant,—something better and more useful than it was before; the plant passes into an animal—a step higher still. And, therefore, we may be sure that the same rule will hold good about us men and women, that when we die, we shall begin a new and a nobler life, that is, if we have been true *men*; if we have lived fulfilling the law of our kind. St. Paul tells us so positively. He says that nothing comes to life except it first die, then God gives it a new body. He says that even so is the resurrection of the dead,—that we gain a step by dying; that we are sown in corruption, and are raised in incorruption; we are sown in dishonour, and are raised in glory; we are sown in weakness, and are raised in power; we are sown a natural body, and are raised a spiritual body; that as we now are of the earth earthy, after death and the resurrection our new and nobler body will be of the heavens heavenly; so that "when this corruptible shall have put on incorruption, and this mortal shall have put on immortality, then death shall be swallowed up in victory." Therefore, I say, Sorrow not for those who sleep as if you had no hope for the dead; for "Christ is risen from the dead, and become the first-fruits of them that slept. For as in Adam all die, even so in Christ shall all be made alive."

And I say that this has to do with the text—it has to do with Ascension-day. For if we claim our share in Christ,—if we claim our share of our heavenly Father's promise, "to give the Holy Spirit to those who ask Him;" then we may certainly hope for our share in Christ's resurrection, our share in Christ's ascension. For, says St. Paul (Rom. viii. 10, 11), "if Christ be in you, the body is dead because of sin, but the Spirit is life because of righteousness. But if the Spirit of Him who raised up Jesus from the dead dwell in you, He that raised up Christ from the dead shall also quicken your mortal bodies, by His Spirit that dwelleth in you!" There is a blessed promise! that in that, as in every thing, we shall be made like Christ our Master, the new Adam, who is a life-giving Spirit, that as He was brought to life again by the Spirit of God, so we shall be. And so will be fulfilled in us the glorious rule which the text lays down, "Thou, O God, sendest forth Thy Spirit, and they are created, and Thou dost renew the face of the earth." Fulfilled?—yes, but far more gloriously than ever the old Psalmist expected. Read the Revelations of St. John, chapters xxi. and xxii. for the glory of the renewed earth read the first Epistle of Paul to the Thessalonians, chap. iv. 16–18, for the glorious resurrection and ascension of those who have died trusting in the blessed Lord, who died for them; and then see what a glorious future lies before us—see how death is but the gate of life—see how what holds true of every thing on this earth, down to the flint beneath our feet, holds true ten thousand times of men that to die and to decay is only to pass into a nobler state of life. But remember, that just as we are better than the stone, we may be also worse than the stone. It cannot disobey God's laws, therefore it can enjoy no reward, any more than suffer any punishment. We can disobey—we can fall from our calling—we can cast God's law behind us—we can refuse to do His will, to work out our own salvation; and just because our reward in the life to come will be so glorious, if we fulfil our life and law, the life of faith and the law of love, therefore will our punishment be so horrible, if we neglect the life of faith and trample under foot the law of love. Oh, my friends, choose! Death is before you all. Shall it be the gate of everlasting life and glory, or the gate of everlasting death and misery? Will you claim your glorious inheritance, and be for ever equal to the angels, doing God's will on earth as they in heaven; or will you fall lower than the stones, who, at all events, must do their duty as stones, and not *do* God's will at all, but only *suffer* it in eternal woe? You must do one or the other. You cannot be like the stones, without feeling—without joy or sorrow, just because you are immortal spirits, every one of you. You must be either happy or miserable, blessed or disgraced, for ever. I know of no middle path;—do you? Choose before the night comes, in which no man can work. Our life is but a vapour which appears for a little time, then vanishes away. "O Lord, how manifold are Thy works! in wisdom hast Thou made them all: the earth is full of Thy riches. That Thou givest them they gather: Thou openest Thine hand, they are filled with good. Thou hidest Thy face, they are troubled: Thou takest away their breath, they die, and return to their dust. Thou sendest forth Thy Spirit, they are created: and Thou renewest the face of the earth."

SERMON IV.
THE WORK OF GOD'S SPIRIT.

JAMES, i. 16, 17.

"Do not err, my beloved brethren; every good gift and every perfect gift is from above, and cometh down from the Father of lights."

THIS text, I believe more and more every day, is one of the most important ones in the whole Bible; and just at this time it is more important for us than ever, because people have forgotten it more than ever.

And, according as you firmly believe this text, according as you firmly believe that every good gift you have in body and soul comes down from above, from God the Father of lights—according, I say, as you believe this, and live upon that belief, just so far will you be able to do your duty to God and man, worthily of your blessed Saviour's calling and redemption, and of the high honour which He has given you of being free and christened men, redeemed by His most precious blood, and led by His most noble Spirit.

Now, just because this text is so important, the devil is particularly busy in trying to make people forget it. For what is his plan? Is it not to make us forget God, to put God *out* of all our thoughts, to make us acknowledge God in none of our ways, to make us look at ourselves and not at God, that so we may become first earthly and sensual, and then devilish, like Satan himself? Therefore he tries to make us disbelieve this text. He puts into our hearts such thoughts as these:—'Ay, all good gifts may come from God; but that only means all spiritual gifts. All those fine, deep doctrines and wonderful feelings that some very religious people talk of, about conversion, and regeneration, and sanctification, and assurance, and the witness of the indwelling Spirit,—all those gifts come from God, no doubt, but they are quite above us. We are straightforward, simple people, who cannot feel fine fancies; if we can be honest, and industrious, and good-natured, and sober, and strong, and healthy, that is enough for us,—and all that has nothing to do with religion. Those are not gifts which come from God. A man is strong and healthy by birth, and honest and good-natured by nature. Those are very good things; but they are not gifts—they are not *graces*—they are not *spiritual* blessings—they have nothing to do with the state of a man's soul. Ungodly people are honest, and good-tempered, and industrious, and healthy, as well as your saints and your methodists; so what is the use of praying for spiritual gifts to God, when we can have all we want by nature?'

Did such thoughts never come into your head, my friends? Are they not often in your heads, more or less? Perhaps not in these very words, but something like them.

I do not say it to blame you, for I believe that every man, each according to his station, is tempted to such thoughts; I believe that such thoughts are not *yours* or any man's; I believe they are the devil's, who tempts all men, who tempted even the Son of God Himself with thoughts like these at their root. Such thoughts are not *yours* or mine, though they may come into our heads. They are part of the evil which besets us—which is *not* us—which has no right or share in us—which we pray God to drive away from us when we say, "Deliver us from evil." Have you not all had such thoughts? But have you not all had very different thoughts? have you not, every one of you, at times, felt in the bottom of your hearts, after all, 'This strength and industry, this courage, and honesty, and good-nature of mine, must come from God; I did not get them myself? If I was born honest, and strong, and gentle, and brave, some one must have made me so when I was born, or before? The devil certainly did not make me so, therefore *God* must? These, too, are His gifts?'

Did you ever think such thoughts as these? If you did not, not much matter, for you have all acted, more or less, in your better moments as if you had them. There are more things in a man's heart, thank God, than ever come into his head. Many a man does a noble thing by instinct, as we say, without ever *thinking* whether it is a noble thing or not—without *thinking* about it at all. Many a man, thank God, is led at times, by God's Spirit, without ever knowing whose Spirit it is that leads him.

But he *ought* to know it, for it is *willing, reasonable* service which God wants of us. He does not care to use us like tools and puppets. And why? He is not merely our Maker, He is our Father, and He wishes us to know and feel that we are His children—to know and feel that we all have come from Him; to acknowledge Him in all our ways, to thank Him for all, to look up lovingly and confidently to Him for more, as His reasonable children, day by day, and hour by hour. Every good gift we have comes from Him; but He will have us know where they all come from.

Let us go through now a few of these good gifts, which we call natural, and see what the Bible says of them, and from whom they come.

First, now, that common gift of strength and courage. Who gives you that?—who gave it David? For He that gives it to one is most likely to be He that gives it to another. David says to God, "Thou teachest my hands to war, and my fingers to fight; by the help of God I can leap over a wall: He makes me strong, that my arms can break even a bow of steel:"—that is plain-spoken enough, I think. Who gave Samson his strength, again? What says the Bible? How Samson met a young lion which roared against him, and he had nothing in his hand, and the Spirit of the Lord came mightily upon him, and he tore the lion as he would have torn a kid. And, again, how when traitors had bound him with two new cords, the Spirit of the Lord came mightily upon him, and the cords which were on his arms became as flax that was burnt with fire, and fell from off his hands. And, for God's sake, do not give in to that miserable fancy that because these stories are what you call miraculous, therefore they have nothing to do with you—that Samson's strength came to him miraculously by God's Spirit, and yet yours comes to you a different way. The Bible is written to tell you how all that happens really happens—what all things really are; God is working among us always, but we do not see Him; and the Bible just lifts up, once and for all, the veil which hides Him from us, and lets us see, in one instance, who it is that does all the wonderful things which go on round us to this day, that when we see any thing like it happen we may know whom to thank for it.

The Great Physician healed the blind and the lame in Judea; and why?—to shew us who heals the blind and the lame now—to shew us that the good gift of medicine and surgery, and the physician's art, comes down from Him who cured the paralytic and cleansed the lepers in Judea—to whom all power is given in heaven and earth.

So, again, with skill in farming and agriculture. From whom does that come? The very heathens can tell us that, for it is curious, that among the heathen, in all ages and countries, those men who have found out great improvements in tilling the ground have been honoured and often worshipped as divine men—as gods, thereby shewing that the heathen, among all their idolatries, had a true and just notion about man's practical skill and knowledge—that it could only come from Heaven, that it was by the inspiration and guidance of God above that skill in agriculture arose. What says Isaiah of that to the very same purpose? "Doth the ploughman plow all day to sow? doth he open and break the clods of his ground? When he hath made plain the face thereof, doth he not cast abroad the vetches, and cast in the principal wheat and the appointed barley and the rye in their place? For his God doth instruct him to discretion, and doth teach him. This also," says Isaiah, "cometh from the Lord of Hosts, who is wonderful in counsel, and excellent in working." Would to God you would all believe it!

Again; wisdom and prudence, and a clear, powerful mind,—are not they parts of God's likeness? How is God's Spirit described in Scripture? It is called the Spirit of wisdom and understanding, the Spirit of prudence and might. Therefore, surely, all wisdom and understanding, all prudence and strength of mind, are, like that Spirit, part of God's image; and where did we get God's image? Can we make ourselves like God? If we are like him, He must have formed that likeness; and He alone. The Spirit of God, says the Scripture, giveth us understanding.

Or, again; good-nature and affection, love, generosity, pity,—whose likeness are they? What is God's name but love? God is love. Has not He revealed Himself as the God of mercy, full of long-suffering, compassion, and free forgiveness; and must not, then, all love and affection, all compassion and generosity, be His gift? Yes. As the rays come from the sun, and yet are not the sun, even so our love and pity, though they are not God, but merely a poor, weak image and reflection of Him, yet from Him alone they come. If there is mercy in our hearts, it comes from the fountain of mercy. If there is the light of love in us, it is a ray from the full sun of His love.

Or honesty, again, and justice,—whose image are they but God's? Is He not THE Just One—the righteous God? Is not what is just for man just for God? Are not the laws of justice and honesty, by which man deals fairly with man, *His* laws—the laws by which God deals with us? Does not every book—I had almost said every page—in the Bible shew us that all our justice is but the pattern and copy of God's justice,—the working out of those six latter commandments of His, which are summed up in that one command, "Thou shalt love thy neighbour as thyself?"

Now here, again, I ask: If justice and honesty be God's likeness, who made us like God in this—who put into us this sense of justice which all have, though so few obey it? Can man make himself like God? Can a worm ape his Maker? No. From God's Spirit, the Spirit of Right, came this inborn feeling of justice, this knowledge of right and wrong, to us—part of the image of God in which He created man—part of the breath or spirit of life which He breathed into Adam. Do not mistake me. I do not say that the sense, and honesty, and love in us, *are* God's Spirit—they are the spirit of *man*, but that they are *like* God's Spirit, and therefore they must be given us *by* God's Spirit to be used as God's Spirit Himself uses them. How a man shall have his share of God's Spirit, and live in and by God's Spirit, is another question, and a higher and more blessed one; but we must master this question first— we must believe that our spirits come *from* God, then, perhaps, we shall begin to see that our spirits never can work well unless they are joined to the Spirit of God, from whom they came. From whom else, I ask again, can they come? Can they come from our bodies? Our bodies? What are they?— Flesh and bones, made up of air and water and earth,—out of the dead bodies of the animals, the dead roots and fruits of plants which we eat. They are earth—matter. Can *matter* be courageous? Did you ever hear of a good-natured plant, or an honest stone? Then this good-nature, and honesty, and courage of ours, must belong to our souls—our spirits. Who put them there? Did we? Does a child make its own character? Does its body make its character first? Can its father and mother make its character? No. Our characters must come from some spirit above us—either from God or from the devil. And is the devil likely to make us honest, or brave, or kindly? I leave you to answer that. God—God alone, my friends, is the author of good—the help that is done on earth, He doeth it all Himself: every good gift and every perfect gift cometh from Him.

Now some of you may think this a strange sort of sermon, because I have said little or nothing about Jesus Christ and His redemption in it, but I say—No.

You must believe this much about yourselves before you can believe more. You must fairly and really believe that *God* made you one thing before you can believe that you have made yourselves another thing. You must really believe that you are not mere machines and animals, but immortal souls, before you can really believe that you have sinned; for animals cannot sin—only reasonable souls can sin. We must really believe that God made us at bottom in His likeness, before we can begin to find out that there is another likeness in us besides God's—a selfish, brutish, too often a devilish likeness, which must be repented of, and fought against, and cast out, that God's likeness in us may get the upper hand, and we may be what God expects us to be. We must know our dignity before we can feel our shame. We must see how high we have a right to stand, that we may see how low, alas! we have fallen.

Now you—I know many such here, thank God—to whom God has given clear, powerful heads for business, and honest, kindly hearts, I do beseech you—consider my words, Who has given you these but God? They are talents which He has committed to your charge; and will He not require an account of them? *He* only, and His free mercy, has made you to differ from others; if you are better than the fools and profligates round you, He, and not yourselves, has made you better. What have you that you have not received? By the grace of God alone you are what you are. If good comes easier to you than to others, *He* alone has made it easier to you; and if you have done wrong,—if you have fallen short of your duty, as *all* fall short, is not your sin greater than others? for unto whom much is given of them shall much be required. Consider that, for God's sake, and see if you, too, have not something to be ashamed of, between yourselves and God. See if you, too, have not need of Jesus Christ and His precious blood, and God's free forgiveness, who have had so much light and power given you, and still have fallen short of what you might have been, and what, by God's grace, you still may be, and, as I hope and earnestly pray, still will be.

And you, young men and women—consider;—if God has given you manly courage and high spirits, and strength and beauty—think—*God*, your Father, has given them to you, and of them He will surely require an account;

therefore, "Rejoice, young people," says Solomon, "in your youth, and let your hearts cheer you in the days of your youth, and walk in the ways of your heart and in the sight of your eyes. But remember," continues the wisest of men,—"remember, that for all these things God shall bring you into judgment." Now do not misunderstand that. It does not mean that there is a sin in being happy. It does not mean, that if God has given to a young man a bold spirit and powerful limbs, or to a young woman a handsome face and a merry, loving heart, that He will punish them for these—God forbid! what He gives He means to be used: but this it means, that according as you use those blessings so will you be judged at the last day; that for them, too, you will be brought to judgment, and tried at the bar of God. As you have used them for industry, and innocent happiness, and holy married love, or for riot and quarrelling, and idleness, and vanity, and filthy lusts, so shall you be judged. And if any of you have sinned in any of these ways,—God forbid that you should have sinned in *all* these ways; but surely, surely, some of you have been idle—some of you have been riotous—some of you have been vain—some of you have been quarrelsome—some of you, alas! have been that which I shall not name here.—Think, if you have sinned in any one of these ways, how can you answer it to God? Have you no need of forgiveness? Have you no need of the blessed Saviour's blood to wash you clean? Young people! God has given you much. As a young man, I speak to you. Youth is an inestimable blessing or an inestimable curse, according as you use it; and if you have abused your spring-time of youth, as all, I am afraid, have—as I have—as almost all do, alas! in this fallen world, where can you get forgiveness but from Him that died on the cross to take away the sins of the world?

SERMON V.
FAITH.

HABAKKUK, ii. 4.

"The just shall live by faith."

THIS is those texts of which there are so many in the Bible, which, though they were spoken originally to one particular man, yet are meant for every man. These words were spoken to Habakkuk, a Jewish prophet, to check him for his impatience under God's hand; but they are just as true for every man that ever was and ever will be as they were for him. They are world-wide and world-old; they are the law by which all goodness, and strength, and safety, stand either in men or angels, for it always was true, and always must be true, that if reasonable beings are to live at all, it is by faith.

And why? Because every thing that is, heaven and earth, men and angels, are all the work of God—of one God, infinite, almighty, all-wise, all-loving, unutterably glorious. My friends, we do not think enough of this,—not that all the thinking in the world can ever make us comprehend the majesty of our Heavenly Father; but we do not remember enough what we *do* know of God. We think of God, watching the world and all things in it, and keeping them in order as a shepherd does his sheep, and so far so good; but we forget that God does more than this,—we forget that this earth, sun, and moon, and all the thousand thousand stars which cover the midnight sky,—many of them suns larger than the sun we see, and worlds larger than the world on which we stand, that all these, stretching away millions of millions of miles into boundless space,—all are lying, like one little grain of dust, in the hollow of God's hand, and that if He were to shut His hand upon them, He could crush them into nothing, and God would be alone in the universe again, as He was before heaven and earth were made. Think of that!—that if God was but to will it, we, and this earth on which we stand, and the heaven above us, and the sun that shines on us, should vanish away, and be no-where and no-thing. Think of the infinite power of God, and then think how is it possible to *live*, except by faith in Him, by trusting to Him utterly.

If you accustom yourselves to think in the same way of the infinite wisdom of God, and the infinite love of God, they will both teach you the same lesson; they will shew you that if you were the greatest, the wisest, the holiest man that ever lived, you would still be such a speck by the side of the Almighty and Everlasting God that it would be madness to depend upon yourselves for any thing while you lived in God's world. For, after all, what *can* we do without God? *In* Him we live, and move, and have our being. He made us, He gave us our bodies, gave us our life; what we do *He* lets us do, what we say He lets us say; we all live on sufferance. What is it but God's infinite mercy that ever brought us here or keeps us here an instant? We may pretend to act without God's leave or help, but it is impossible for us to do so; the strength we put forth, the wit we use, are all His gifts. We cannot draw a breath of air without His leave. And yet men fancy they can do without God in the world! My friends, these are but few words, and poor words, about the glorious majesty of God and our littleness when compared with Him; but I have said quite enough, at least, to shew you all how absurd it is to depend upon ourselves for any thing. If we are mere creatures of God, if God alone has every blessing both of this world and the next, and the will to give them away, whom *are* we to go to but to Him for all we want? It is so in the life of our bodies, and it is so in the life of our spirits. If we wish for God's blessings, from God we must ask them. That is our duty, even though God in His mercy and long-suffering does pour down many a blessing upon men who never trust in Him for them. To us all, indeed, God gives blessings before we are old enough to trust in Him for them, and to many He continues those blessings in after-life in spite of their blindness and want of faith. "He maketh His sun to shine on the evil and on the good, and sendeth rain on the just and on the unjust." He gives—gives—it is His glory to give. Yet strange! that men will go on year after year, using the limbs, and eating the food, which God gives them, without ever believing so much as that God *has* given them, without so much as looking up to heaven once and saying, "God, I thank Thee!" But we must remember that those blessings will not last for ever. Unless a man has lived by faith in God with regard to his earthly comforts, death will come and put an end to them at once; and then it is only those who have trusted in God for all good things, and thanked Him accordingly in this life, who shall have their part in the new heavens and the new earth, which will so immeasurably surpass all that this earth can give.

And it is the same with the life of our spirits; in it, too, we must live by faith. The life of our spirits is a gift from God the Father of spirits, and He has chosen to declare that unless we trust to Him for life, and ask Him for life, He will not bestow it upon us. The life of our bodies He in His mercy keeps up, although we forget Him; the life of our souls He will not keep up: therefore, for the sake of our spirits, even more than of our bodies, we must live by faith. If we wish to be loving, pure, wise, manly, noble, we must ask those excellent gifts of God, who is Himself infinite love, and purity, wisdom and nobleness. If we wish for everlasting life, from whom can we obtain it but from God, who is the boundless, eternal, life itself? If we wish for forgiveness for our faults and failings, where are we to get it but from God, who is boundless love and pity, and who has revealed to us His boundless love and pity in the form of a man, Jesus Christ the Saviour of the world?

And to go a step further; it is by faith in Christ we must live—in Christ, a man like ourselves, yet God blessed for ever. For it is a certain truth, that men cannot believe in God or trust in Him unless they can think of Him as a man. This was the reason why the poor heathen made themselves idols in the form of men, that they might have something like themselves to worship; and those among them who would not worship idols almost always ended in fancying that God was either a mere notion, or else a mere part of this world, or else that He sat up in heaven neither knowing nor caring what happened upon earth. But we, to whom God has given the glorious news of His Gospel, have the very Person to worship whom all the heathen were searching after and could not find,—one who is "very God," infinite in love, wisdom, and strength, and yet "very man," made in all points like ourselves, but without sin; so that we have not a High Priest who cannot be touched with the feeling of our infirmities, but one who is able to help those who are tempted, because He was tempted Himself like us, and overcame by the strength of His own perfect will, of His own perfect faith. By trusting in Him, and acknowledging Him in every thought and action of our lives, we shall be safe, for it is written, "The just shall live by faith."

These things are true, and always were true. All that men ever did well, or nobly, or lovingly, in this world, *was done by faith*—by faith in God of some sort or other; even in the man who thinks least about religion, it is so. Every time a man means to do, and really does, a just or generous action, he does it because he believes, more or less clearly, that there is a just and loving God above him, and that justice and love are the right thing for a man—the law by which God intended him to walk: so that this small, dim faith still shews itself in practice; and the more faith a man has in God and in God's laws, the more it will shew itself in every action of his daily life; and the more this faith works in his life and conduct, the better man he is;—the more he is like God's image, in which man was originally made;—and the more he is like Christ, the new pattern of God's image, whom all men must copy.

So that the sum of the matter is this, without Christ we can do nothing, by trusting in Christ we can do every thing. See, then, how true the verse before my text must be, that he whose soul is lifted up in him is not upright; for if a man fancies that his body and soul are his own, to do what he pleases with them, when all the time they are God's gift;—if a man fancies that he can take perfect care of himself, while all the time it is God that is keeping him out of a thousand sins and dangers;—if a man fancies that he can do right of himself, when all the time the little good that he does is the work of God's Spirit, which has not yet left him;—if a man fancies, in short, that he can do without God, when all the time it is in God that he lives, and moves, and has his being, how can such a man be called upright? Upright! he is utterly wrong;—he is believing a lie, and walking accordingly; and, therefore, instead of keeping upright, he is going where all lies lead; into all kinds of low and crooked ways, mistakes, absurdities, and at last to ruin of body and soul. Nothing but truth can keep a man upright and straight, can keep a man where God has put him, and where he ought to be; and the man whose heart is puffed up by pride and self-conceit, who is looking at himself and not at God, that man has begun upon a falsehood, and will soon get out of tune with heaven and earth. For consider, my friends: suppose some rich and mighty prince went out and collected a number of children, and of sick and infirm people, and said to them, "You cannot work now, but I will give you food, medicine, every thing that you require, and then you must help me to work; and I, though you have no right to expect it of me, will pay you for the little work you can do on the strength of my food and medicine."—Is it not plain that all those persons could only live by faith in their prince, by trusting in him for food and medicine, and by acknowledging that that food and medicine came from him, and thanking him accordingly? If they wished to be true men, if they wished him to continue his bounty, they would confess that all the health and strength they had belonged to him of right, because his generosity had given it to them. Just in this position we stand with Christ the Lord. When the whole world lay in wickedness, He came and chose us, of His free grace and mercy, to be one of His peculiar nations, to work for Him and with Him; and from the time He came, all that we and our forefathers have done well has been done by the strength and wisdom which Christ has given us. Now suppose, again, that one of the persons of whom I spoke was seized with a fit of pride—suppose he said to himself, "My health and strength does not come from the food and medicine which the prince gave me, it comes from the goodness of my own constitution; the wages which I am paid are my just due, I am a free man, and may choose what master I like." Suppose any one of *your* servants treated you so, would you not be inclined to answer, "You are a faithless, ungrateful fellow; go your ways, then, and see how little you can do without my bounty?" But the blessed King in heaven, though He is provoked every day, is more long-suffering than man. All He does is to withdraw His bounty for a moment, to take this world's blessings from a man, and let him find out how impossible it is for him to keep himself out of affliction—to take away His Holy Spirit for a moment from a man, and let him see how straight he rushes astray, and every way but the right; and then, if the man is humbled by his fall or his affliction, and comes back to his Lord, confessing how weak he is and promising to trust in Christ and thank Christ only for the future, *then* our Lord will restore His blessings to him, and there will be joy among the angels of God over one sinner that repents. This was the way in which God treated Job when, in spite of all his excellence, *his* heart was lifted up. And then, when he saw his own folly, and abhorred himself, and repented in dust and ashes, God restored to him sevenfold what He had taken from him— honour, wisdom, riches, home, and children. This is the way, too, in which God treated David. "In my prosperity," he tells us, "I said, I shall never be moved; thou, Lord, of Thy goodness hast made my hill so strong"—forgetting that he must be kept safe every moment of his life, as well as made safe once for all. "Thou didst turn Thy face from me, and I was troubled. Then cried I unto Thee, O Lord, and gat me to my Lord right humbly. And THEN," he adds, "God turned my heaviness into joy, and girded me with gladness," (Psalm xxx.) And again, he says, "*Before* I was troubled I went wrong, but *now* I have kept Thy word," (Psalm cxix.) And this is the way in which Christ the Lord treated St. Peter and St. Paul, and treats, in His great mercy, every Christian man when He sees him puffed up, to bring him to his senses, and make him live by faith in God. If he takes the warning, well; if he does not, he remains in a lie, and must go where all lies lead. So perfectly does it hold throughout a man's whole life, that he whose soul is lifted up within him is not upright; but that the just must live by faith.

Now there is one objection apt to rise in men's minds when they hear such words as these, which is, that they take such a "low view of human nature;" it is so galling to our pride to be told that we can do nothing for ourselves: but if we think of the matter more closely, and, above all, if we try to put it into practice and live by faith, we shall find that there is no real reason for thus objecting. This is not a doctrine which ought to make us despise men; any doctrine that *does*, does not come of *God*. Men are not contemptible creatures—they are glorious creatures—they were created in the image of God; God has put such honour upon them that He has given them dominion over the whole earth, and made them partakers of His eternal reason; and His Spirit gives them understanding to enable them to conquer this earth, and make the beasts, ay, and the very winds and seas, and fire and steam, their obedient servants; and human nature, too, when it is what God made it, and what it ought to be, is not a contemptible thing: it was noble enough for the Son of God to take it upon Himself—to become man, without sinning or defiling Himself; and what was good enough for Him is surely good enough for us. Wickedness consists in *unmanliness*, in being unlike a man, in becoming like an evil spirit or a beast. Holiness consists in becoming a *true man*, in becoming more and more like the likeness of Jesus Christ. And when the Bible tells us that we can do nothing of ourselves, but can live only by faith, the Bible puts the highest honour upon us which any created thing can have. What are the things which cannot live by faith? The trees and plants, the beasts and birds, which, though they live and grow by God's providence, yet do not know it, do not thank Him, cannot ask Him for more strength and life as we can, are mere dead tools in God's hands, instead of living, reasonable beings as we are. It is only reasonable beings, like men and angels, with immortal spirits in them, who *can* live by faith; and it is the greatest glory and honour to us, I say again, that we *can* do so—that the glorious, infinite God, Maker of heaven and earth, should condescend to ask us to be loyal to Him, to love Him, should encourage us to pray to Him boldly, and then should condescend to hear our prayers—*we*, who in comparison of Him are smaller than the gnats in the sunbeam in comparison of men! And then, when we remember that He has sent His only Son into the world to take our nature upon Him, and join us all together into one great and everlasting family, the body of Christ the Lord, and that He has actually given us a share in His own Almighty Holy Spirit that we may be able to love Him, and to serve Him, and to be joined to Him, the Almighty Father, do we not see that all this is infinitely more honourable to us than if we were each to go on his own way here without God—without knowing anything of the everlasting world of spirits to which we now belong? My friends, instead of being ashamed of being able to do nothing for ourselves, we ought to rejoice at having God for our Father and our Friend, to enable us to "do all things through Him who strengthens us"—to do whatever is noble, and loving, and worthy of true men. Instead, then, of dreaming conceitedly that God will accept us for our own sakes, let us just be content to be accepted for the sake of Jesus Christ our King. Instead of trying to walk through this world without God's help, let us ask God to help and guide us in every action of our lives, and then go manfully forward, doing with all our might whatsoever our hands or our hearts see right to do, trusting to God to put us in the right path, and to fill our heads with right thoughts and our hearts with right feeling; and so our faith will shew itself in our works, and we shall be justified at the last day, as all good men have ever been, by trusting to our Heavenly Father and to the Lord Jesus Christ, and the guidance of His Holy Spirit.

SERMON VI.
THE SPIRIT AND THE FLESH.

Galatians, v. 16.

"I say then, Walk in the Spirit, and ye shall not fulfil the lusts of the flesh. For the flesh lusteth against the Spirit, and the Spirit against the flesh, and these are contrary the one to the other."

The more we think seriously, my friends, the more we shall see what wonderful and awful things words are, how they mean much more than we fancy,—how we do not make words, but words are given to us by one higher than ourselves. Wise men say that you can tell the character of any nation by its language, by watching the words they use, the names they give to things, for out of the abundance of the heart the mouth speaks, and by our words, our Lord tells us, we shall be justified and condemned.

It is God, and Christ, the Word of God, who gives words to men, who puts it into the hearts of men to call certain things by certain names; and, according to a nation's godliness, and wisdom, and purity of heart, will be its power of using words discreetly and reverently. That miracle of the gift of tongues, of which we read in the New Testament, would have been still most precious and full of meaning if it had had no other use than this—to teach men from whom words come. When men found themselves all of a sudden inspired to talk in foreign languages which they had never learnt, to utter words of which they themselves did not know the meaning, do you not see how it must have made them feel that all language is God's making and God's giving? Do you not see how it must have made them feel what awful, mysterious things words were, like those cloven tongues of fire which fell on the apostles? The tongues of fire signified the difficult foreign languages which they suddenly began to speak as the Spirit gave them utterance. And where did the tongues of fire come from? Not out of themselves, not out of the earth beneath, but down from the heaven above, to signify that it is not from man, from man's flesh or brain, or the earthly part of him, that words are bred, but that they come down from Christ the Word of God, and are breathed into the minds of men by the Spirit of God. Why do I speak of all this? To make you feel what awful, wonderful things words are; how, when you want to understand the meaning of a word, you must set to work with reverence and godly fear—not in self-conceit and prejudice, taking the word to mean just what suits your own notions of things, but trying humbly to find out what the word really does mean of itself, what God meant it to mean when He put it into the hearts of wise men to use that word and bring it into our English language. A man ought to read a newspaper or a story-book in that spirit; how much more, when he takes up the Bible! How reverently he ought to examine every word in the New Testament—this very text, for instance. We ought to be sure that St. Paul, just because he was an inspired apostle, used the very best possible words to express what he meant on so important a matter; and what *are* the best words? The clearest and the simplest words are the best words; else how is the Bible to be the poor man's book? How, unless the wayfaring man, though simple, shall not err therein? Therefore we may be sure the words in Scripture are certain to be used in their simplest, most natural, most everyday meaning, such as the simplest man can understand. And, therefore, we may be sure, that these two words, "flesh" and "spirit," in my text, are used in their very simplest, straightforward sense; and that St. Paul meant by them what working-men mean by them in the affairs of daily life. No doubt St. Peter says that there are many things in St. Paul's writings difficult to be understood, which those who are unlearned and unstable wrest to their own destruction; and, most true it is, so they do daily. But what does "wresting" a thing mean? It means twisting it, bending it, turning it out of its original straightforward, natural meaning, into some new crooked meaning of their own. This is the way we are all of us too apt, I am afraid, to come to St. Paul's Epistles. We find him difficult because we won't take him at his word, because we tear a text out of its right place in the chapter—the place where St. Paul put it, and make it stand by itself, instead of letting the rest of the chapter explain its meaning. And then, again, people use the words in the text as unfairly and unreasonably as they use the text itself, they won't let the words have their common-sense English meaning—they must stick a new meaning on them of their own. 'Oh,' they say, 'that text must not be taken literally, that word has a spiritual signification here. Flesh does not mean flesh, it means men's corrupt nature;' little thinking all the while that perhaps they understand those words, spiritual, and corrupt, and nature, just as ill as they do the rest of the text.

How much better, my friends, to let the Bible tell its own story; not to be so exceeding wise above what is written, just to believe that St. Paul knew better how to use words than we are likely to do,—just to believe that when he says flesh he means flesh. Everybody agrees that when he says spirit he means spirit, why, in the name of common sense, when he says flesh should he not mean flesh? For my own part I believe that when St. Paul talks of man's flesh, he means by it man's body, man's heart and brain, and all his bodily appetites and powers—what we call a man's constitution; in a word, the *animal* part of man, just what a man has in common with the beasts who perish.

To understand what I mean, consider any animal—a dog, for instance—how much every animal has in it what men have,—a body, and brain, and heart;

it hungers and thirsts as we do, it can feel pleasure and pain, anger and loneliness, and fear and madness; it likes freedom, company, and exercise, praise and petting, play and ease; it uses a great deal of cunning, and thought, and courage, to get itself food and shelter, just as human beings do: in short, it has a fleshly nature, just as we have, and yet, after all, it is but an animal, and so, in one sense, we are all animals, only more delicately made than the other animals; but we are something more, we have a spirit as well as a flesh, an immortal soul. If any one asks, what is a man? the true answer is, an animal with an immortal spirit in it; and this spirit can feel more than pleasure and pain, which are mere carnal, that is, fleshly things; it can feel trust, and hope, and peace, and love, and purity, and nobleness, and independence, and, above all, it can feel right and wrong. There is the infinite difference between an animal and a man, between our flesh and our spirit; an animal has no sense of right and wrong; a dog who has done wrong is often terrified, but not because he feels it wrong and wicked, but because he knows from experience that he will be punished for doing it: just so with a man's fleshly nature;—a carnal, fleshly man, a man whose spirit is dead within him, whose spiritual sense of right and wrong, and honour and purity, is gone, when he has done a wrong thing is often enough afraid; but why? Not for any spiritual reason, not because he feels it a wicked and abominable thing, a sin, but because he is afraid of being punished for it, because he is afraid that his body, his flesh will be punished by the laws of the land, or by public opinion, or because he has some dim belief that this same body and flesh of his will be burnt in hell-fire; and fire, he knows by experience, is a painful thing—and so he is *afraid* of it; there is nothing spiritual in all that,—that is all fleshly, carnal; the heathens in all ages have been afraid of hell-fire; but a man's spirit, on the other hand, if it be in hell, is in a very different hell from mere fire,—a spiritual hell, such as torments the evil spirits, at this very moment, although they are going to and fro on this very earth. This earth is hell to them; they carry about hell in them,—they are their own hell. Everlasting shame, discontent, doubt, despair, rage, disgust at themselves, feeling that they are out of favour with God, out of tune with heaven and earth, loving nothing, believing nothing, ever hating, hating each other, hating themselves most of all—*there* is their hell! *There* is the hell in which the soul of every wicked man is,—ay, is now while he is in *this* life, though he will only awake to the perfect misery of it after death, when his body and fleshly nature have mouldered away in the grave, and can no longer pamper and stupify him and make him forget his own misery. Ay, there has been many a man in this life who had every fleshly enjoyment which this world can give, riches and pleasure, banquets and palaces, every sense and every appetite pampered,—his pride and his vanity flattered; who never knew what want, or trouble, or contradiction, was on the smallest point; a man, I say, who had every carnal enjoyment which this earth can give to a man's selfish flesh, and yet whose spirit was in hell all the while, and who knew it; hating and despising himself for a mean selfish villain, while all the world round was bowing down to him and envying him as the luckiest of men. I am trying to make you understand the infinite difference between a man's flesh and his spirit; how a man's flesh can take no pleasure in spiritual things, while man's spirit of itself can take no pleasure in fleshly things. Now, the spirit and the flesh, body and soul, in every man, are at war with each other,—they have quarrelled; that is the corruption of our nature, the fruit of Adam's fall. And as the Article says, and as every man who has ever tried to live godly well knows, from experience, "that infection of nature does remain to the last, even in those who are regenerate." So that as St. Paul says, the spirit lusteth against the flesh, and the flesh against the spirit; and it continually happens that a man cannot do the things which he would; he cannot do what he knows to be right; thus, as St. Paul says again, a man may delight in the law of God in his inward man, that is, in his spirit, and yet all the while he shall find another law in his members, *i.e.* in his body, in his flesh, in his brain which thinks, and his heart which feels, and his senses which are fond of pleasure; and this law of the flesh, these appetites and passions which he has, like other animals, fight against the law of his mind, and when he wishes to do good, make him do evil. Now how is this? The flesh is not evil; a man's body can be no more wicked than a dumb beast can be wicked. St. Paul calls man's flesh sinful flesh; not because our flesh can sin of itself, but because our sinful souls make our flesh do sinful things; for, he says, Christ came in the likeness of sinful flesh, and yet in him was no sin. The pure and spotless Saviour could not have taken man's flesh upon him if there was any sinfulness in it. The body knows nothing of right and wrong; it is not subject to the law of God, neither, indeed, can be, says St. Paul. And why? Because God's law is spiritual; deals with right and wrong. Wickedness, like righteousness, is a spiritual thing. If a man sins, his body is not in fault; it is his spirit; his weak, perverse will, which will sooner listen to what his flesh tells him is pleasant than to what God tells him is right; for this, my friends, is the secret of the battle of life. We stand between heaven and earth. Above is God's Spirit striving with our spirits, speaking to them in the depths of our soul, shewing us what is right, putting into our hearts good desires, making us long to be honest and just, pure and manful, loving and charitable; for who is there who has not at times longed after these things, and felt that it would be a blessed thing for him if he were such a man as Jesus Christ was and is?—Above us, I say, is God's Spirit speaking to our spirits, below us is this world speaking to our flesh, as it spoke to Eve's, saying to us, "This thing is pleasant to the eyes—this thing is good for food—that thing is to be desired to make you wise, and to flatter your vanity and self-conceit." Below us, I say, is *this* world, tempting us to ease, and pleasure, and vanity; and in the middle, betwixt the two, stands up the third part of man—his *soul* and *will*, set to choose between the voice of God's Spirit and the temptations of this world—to choose between what is right and what is pleasant—to choose whether he will obey the desires of the spirit, or obey the desires of the flesh. He must choose. If he lets his flesh conquer his spirit, he falls; if he lets his spirit conquer his flesh, he rises; if he lets his flesh conquer his spirit, he becomes what he was not meant to be—a slave to fleshly lust; and *then* he will find his flesh set up for itself, and work for itself. And where man's flesh gets the upper hand, and takes possession of him, it can do nothing but evil—not that it is evil in itself, but that it has no rule, no law to go by; it does not know right from wrong; and therefore it does simply what it likes, as a dumb beast or an idiot might; and therefore the works of the flesh are—adulteries, drunkenness, murders, fornications, envyings, backbitings, strife. When a man's body, which God intended to be the servant of his spirit, has become the tyrant of his spirit, it is like an idiot on a king's throne, doing all manner of harm and folly without knowing that it *is* harm and folly. That is not *its* fault. Whose fault is it, then? *Our* fault—the fault of our wills and our souls. Our souls were intended to be the masters of our flesh, to conquer all the weaknesses, defilements of our constitution—our tempers, our cowardice, our laziness, our hastiness, our nervousness, our vanity, our love of pleasure—to listen to our spirits, because our spirits learn from God's Spirit what is right and noble. But if we let our flesh master us, and obey its own blind lusts, we sin against God; and we sin against God doubly; for we not only sin against God's commandments, but we sin against ourselves, who are the image and glory of God.

Believe this, my friends; believe that, because you are all fallen human creatures, there must go on in you this sore life-long battle between your spirit and your flesh—your spirit trying to be master and guide, as it ought to be, and your flesh rebelling, and trying to conquer your spirit and make you a mere animal, like a fox in cunning, a peacock in vanity, or a hog in greedy sloth. But believe, too, that it is your sin and your shame if your spirit does not conquer your flesh—for God has promised to help your spirits. Ask Him, and His Spirit will teach them—fill them with pure, noble hopes, with calm, clear thoughts, and with deep, unselfish love to God and man. He will strengthen your wills, that they may be able to refuse the evil and choose the good. Ask Him, and He will join them to His own Spirit—to the Spirit of Christ, your Master; for he that is joined unto the Lord is one spirit with Him. Ask him, and He will give you the mind of Christ—teach you to see and feel all matters as Christ sees and feels them. Ask Him, and He will give you wisdom to listen to His Spirit when it teaches your spirit, and then you will be able to walk after the spirit, and not obey the lusts of the flesh; and you will be able to crucify the flesh with its passions and lusts, that is, to make it, what it ought to be, a dead thing—a dead tool for your spirit to work with manfully and godly, and not a live tyrant to lead you into brutishness and folly; and then you will find that the fruit of the spirit, of your spirit led by God's Spirit, is really, as St. Paul says, "love, joy, peace, long-suffering, gentleness, honesty"—"whatsoever things are true, whatsoever things are honourable and of good report;" and instead of being the miserable slaves of your own passions, and of the opinions of your neighbours, you will find that where the Spirit of the Lord is, there is liberty, true freedom, not only from your neighbours' sins, but, what is far better, freedom from your own.

These are large words, my friends, and promise mighty things. But I dare speak them to you, for God has spoken to you. These promises God made you at your baptism; these promises I, on the warrant of your baptism, dare make to you again. At your baptism, God gave you the right to call Him your loving Father, to call His Son your Saviour, His Spirit your Sanctifier. And He is not a man, that He should lie; nor the son of man, that He should repent! Try Him, and see whether He will not fulfil His word. Claim His promise, and though you have fallen lower than the brutes, He will make men and women of you. He will be faithful and just to forgive you your sins, and to cleanse you from all unrighteousness.

SERMON VII.
RETRIBUTION.

Numbers, xxxii. 23.

"Be sure your sin will find you out."

The full meaning of this text is, that every sin which a man commits is certain, sooner or later, to come home to him with fearful interest.

Moses gave this warning to two tribes of the Israelites,—to the Reubenites and Gadites, who had promised to go over Jordan, and help their countrymen in war against the heathen, on condition of being allowed to return and settle on the east bank of Jordan, where they then were; but if they broke their promise, and returned before the end of the war, they were to be certain that their sin would find them out; that God would avenge their falsehood on them in some way in their lifetime: in their lifetime, I say, for there is no mention made in this chapter, or in any part of the story, of heaven or hell, or any world to come. And the text has been always taken as a fair warning to all generations of men, that their sin also, even in their lifetimes, will be visited upon them.

Now, it is strange, at first sight, that these texts, which warn men that their sins will be punished in this life, are just the most unpleasant texts in the whole Bible; that men shrink from them more, and shut their eyes to them more than they do to those texts which threaten them with hell-fire and everlasting death. Strange!—that men should be more afraid of being punished in this life for a few years than in the life to come for ever and ever;—and yet not strange if we consider; for to worldly and sinful souls, that life after death and the flames of hell seem quite distant and dim—things of which they know little and believe less, while this world they *do* know, they are quite certain that its good things are pleasant and its bad things unpleasant, and they are thoroughly afraid of losing *them*. Their hearts are where their treasure is, in this world; and a punishment which deprives them of this world's good things hits them home: but their treasure is *not* in heaven, and, therefore, about losing heaven they are by no means so much concerned. And thus they can face the dreadful news that "the wicked shall be turned into hell, and all the people that forget God;" while, as for the news that the wicked shall be recompensed on the earth, that their sins will surely find them out in this life, they cannot face that—they shut their ears to it,— they try to persuade themselves that sin will *pay* them *here*, at all events; and as for hereafter, they shall get off somehow,—they neither know nor care much how.

Yet God's truth remains, and God's truth must be heard; and those who love this world so well must be told, whether they like or not, that every sin which they commit, every mean, every selfish, every foul deed, loses them so much enjoyment in this very present world of which they are so mighty fond. That is God's truth; and I will prove it true from common sense, from Holy Scripture, and *from the witness* of men's own hearts.

Take common sense. Does not common sense tell us that if God made this world, and governs it by righteous and God-like laws, this must be a world in which evil-doing cannot thrive? God made the world better than that, surely! He would be a bad law-giver who made such laws, that it was as well to break them as to keep them. You would call them bad laws, surely! No, God made the world, and not the devil; and the world works by God's laws, and not the devil's; and it inclines towards good, and not towards evil; and he who sins, even in the least, breaks God's laws, acts contrary to the rule and constitution of the world, and will surely find that God's laws will go on in spite of him, and grind him to powder, if he by sinning gets in the way of them. God has no need to go out of His way to punish our evil deeds. Let them alone, and they will punish themselves. Is it not so in every thing? If a tradesman trades badly, or a farmer farms badly, there is no need of lawyers to punish him; he will punish himself. Every mistake he makes will take money out of his pocket; every time he offends against the established rules of trade or agriculture, which are God's laws, he injures himself; and so, be sure, it is in the world at large,—in the world in which men and the souls of men live, and move, and have their being.

Next, to speak of Scripture. I might quote texts innumerable to prove that what I say Scripture says also. Consider but this one thing,—that there is a whole book in the Bible written to prove this one thing,—that our good and bad deeds are repaid us with interest in this life—the Proverbs of Solomon I mean—in which there is little or no mention of heaven or hell, or any world to come. It is all one noble, and awful, and yet cheering sermon on that one text, "The righteous shall be recompensed in the earth, much more the wicked and the sinner,"—put in a thousand different lights; brought home to us a thousand different roads, comes the same everlasting doom,—"Vain man, who thinkest that thou canst live in God's world and yet despise His will, know that, in every smiling, comfortable sin, thou art hatching an adder to sting thee in the days of old age, to poison thy cup of sinful joy, even when it is at thy lips; to haunt thy restless thoughts, and dog thee day and night; to rise up before thee, in the silent, sleepless hours of night, like an angry ghost! An awful foretaste of the doom that is to come; and yet a merciful foretaste, if thou wilt be but taught by the disappointment, the unsatisfied craving, the gnawing shame of a guilty conscience, to see the heinousness of sin, and would turn before it be too late."

What, my friends,—what will you make of such texts as this, "That he who soweth to the flesh shall of the flesh reap corruption?" Do you not see that comes true far too often? Can it help *always* coming true, seeing that God's apostle spoke it? What will you make of this, too, "That the wicked is snared by the working of his own hands;"—"That *evil*"—the evil which we do of its own self—"shall slay the wicked?" What says the whole noble 37th Psalm of David, but that same awful truth of God, that sin is its own punishment?

Why should I go on quoting texts? Look for yourselves, you who fancy that it is only on the other side of the grave that God will trouble Himself about you and your meanness, your profligacy, your falsehood. Look for yourselves in the book of God, and see if there be any writer there,—lawgiver, prophet, psalmist, apostle, up to Christ the Lord Himself,—who does not warn men again and again, that here, on earth, their sins will find them out. Our Saviour, indeed, when on earth, said less about this subject than any of the prophets before Him, or the apostles after Him, and for the best of reasons. The Jews had got rooted in their minds a superstitious notion, that all disease, all sorrow, was the punishment in each case of some particular sin; and thus, instead of looking with pity and loving awe upon the sick and the afflicted, they were accustomed, too often, to turn from them as sinners, smitten of God, bearing in their distress the token of His anger. The blessed One,—He who came to heal the sick and save the lost,—reproved that error more than once. When the disciples fancied a certain poor man's blindness to be a judgment from God, "Neither did he sin," said the Lord, "nor his parents, but that the glory of God might be made manifest in him." And yet, on the other hand, when He healed a certain man of an old infirmity at the pool of Bethesda, what were His words to him? "Go thy way, sin no more, lest a worse thing come unto thee;"—a clear and weighty warning that all his long misery of eight-and-thirty years had been the punishment of some sin of his, and that the sin repeated would bring on him a still severer judgment.

What, again, does the apostle mean, in the Epistle to the Hebrews, when he tells us how God scourges every son whom he receives, and talks of His chastisements, whereof all are partakers. Why do we need chastising if we have nothing which needs mending? And though the innocent *may* sometimes be afflicted to make them strong as well as innocent, and the holy chastened to make them humble as well as holy, yet if the good cannot escape their share of affliction, how will the bad get off? "If the righteous scarcely be saved, where will the ungodly and the sinner appear?" But what use in arguing when you know that my words are true? You *know* that your sins will find you out. Look boldly and honestly into your own hearts. Look through the history of your past lives, and confess to God, at least, that the far greater number of your sorrows have been your own fault; that there is hardly a day's misery which you ever endured in your life of which you might not say, 'If I had listened to the voice of God in my conscience—if I had earnestly considered what my *duty* was—if I had prayed to God to determine my judgment right, I should have been spared this sorrow now?' Am I not right? Those who know most of God and their own souls will agree most with me; those who know little about God and their own souls will agree but hardly with me, for they provoke God's chastisements, and writhe under them for the time, and then go and do the same wrong again, as the wild beast will turn and bite the stone thrown at him without having the sense to see why it was thrown.

Think, again, of your past lives, and answer in God's sight, how many wrong things have you ever done which have *succeeded*, that is, how many sins which you would not be right glad were undone if you could but put back the wheels of Time? They may have succeeded *outwardly*; meanness will succeed so—lies—oppression—theft—adultery—drunkenness—godlessness—they are all pleasant enough while they last, I suppose; and a man may reap what he calls substantial benefits from them in money, and suchlike, and keep that safe enough; but has his sin succeeded? Has it not *found him out?*—found him out never to lose him again? Is he the happier for it? Does he feel freer for it? Does he respect himself the more for it?—No! And even though he may prosper now, yet does there not run though all his selfish pleasure a certain fearful looking forward to a fiery judgment to which he would gladly shut his eyes, but cannot?

Cunning, fair-spoken oppressor of the poor, has not thy sin found thee out? Then be sure it will. In the shame of thine own heart it will find thee out;—in the curses of the poor it will find thee out;—in a friendless, restless, hopeless death-bed, thy covetousness and thy cruelty will glare before thee in their true colours, and thy sin will find thee out!

Profligate woman, who art now casting away thy honest name, thy self-respect, thy womanhood, thy baptism-vows, that thou mayest enjoy the foul pleasures of sin for a season, has not thy sin found thee out? Then be sure it will hereafter, when thou hast become disgusted at thyself and thine own infamy,—and youth, and health, and friends, are gone, and a shameful and despised old age creeps over thee, and death stalks nearer and nearer, and God vanishes further and further off, then thy sin will find thee out!

Foolish, improvident young man, who art wasting the noble strength of youth, and manly spirits which God has given thee on sin and folly, throwing away thine honest earnings in cards and drunkenness, instead of laying them by against a time of need—has not thy sin found thee out? Then be sure it will some day, when thou hast to bring home thy bride to a cheerless, unfurnished house, and there to live from hand to mouth,—without money to provide for her sickness,—without money to give her the means of keeping things neat and comfortable when she is well,—without a farthing laid by against distress, and illness, and old age:—*then* your sin will find you out: then, perhaps, my text,—my words—may come across you as you sigh in vain in your comfortless home, in your impoverished old age, for the money which you wasted in your youth! My friends, my friends, for your own sakes consider, and mend ere that day come, as else it surely will!

And, lastly, you who, without running into any especial sins, as those which the world calls sins, still live careless about religion, without loyalty to Christ the Lord, without any honest attempt, or even wish, to serve the God above you, or to rejoice in remembering that you are His children, working for Him and under Him,—be sure your sin will find you out. When affliction, or sickness, or disappointment come, as come they will, if God has not cast you off;—when the dark day dawns, and your fool's paradise of worldly prosperity is cut away from under your feet, then you will find out your folly—you will find that you have insulted the only Friend who can bring you out of affliction—cast off the only comfort which can strengthen you to bear affliction—forgotten the only knowledge which will enable you to be the wiser for affliction. Then, I say, the sin of your godlessness will find you out; if you do not intend to fall, soured and sickened merely by God's chastisements, either into stupid despair or peevish discontent, you will have to go back, to go back to God and cry, "Father, I have sinned against heaven and before Thee, and am no more worthy to be called Thy son."

Go back at once before it be too late. Find out your sins and mend them—before they find you out, and break your hearts.

SERMON VIII.
SELF-DESTRUCTION.

1 KINGS, xxii. 23.

"The Lord hath put a lying spirit in the mouth of all these thy prophets."

THE chapter from which my text is taken, which is the first lesson for this evening's service, is a very awful chapter, for it gives us an insight into the meaning of that most awful and terrible word—temptation. And yet it is a most comforting chapter, for it shews us how God is long-suffering and merciful, even to the most hardened sinner; how to the last He puts before him good and evil, to choose between them, and warns him to the last of his path, and the ruin to which it leads.

We read of Ahab in the first lesson this morning as a thoroughly wicked man,—mean and weak, cruel and ungodly, governed by his wife Jezebel, a heathen woman, in marrying whom he had broken God's law,—a woman so famous for cruelty and fierceness, vanity and wickedness, that her name is a by-word even here in England now—"as bad as Jezebel," we say to this day. We heard of Ahab in this morning's lesson letting Jezebel murder the righteous Naboth, by perjury and slander, to get possession of his vineyard; and then, instead of shrinking with abhorrence from his wife's iniquity, going down and taking possession of the land which he had gained by her sin. We read of God's curse on him, and yet of God's long-suffering and pardon to him on his repentance. Yet, neither God's curse nor God's mercy seem to have moved him. But he had been always the same. "He did evil," the Bible tells us, "in the sight of the Lord above all that were before him." He deserted the true God for his wife's idols and false gods; and in spite of Elijah's miracle at Carmel—of which you heard last Sunday—by which he proved by fire which was the true God, and in spite of the wonderful victory which God had given him, by means of one of God's prophets, over the Syrians, he still remained an idolater. He would not be taught, nor understand; neither God's threats nor mercies could move him; he went on sinning against light and knowledge; and now his cup was full—his days were numbered, and God's vengeance was ready at the door.

He consulted all his false prophets as to whether or not he should go to attack the Syrians at Ramoth-Gilead. They knew what to say—they knew that their business was to prophesy what would pay them—what would be pleasant to him. They did not care whether what they said was true or not—they lied for the sake of gain, for the Lord had put a lying spirit into their mouths. They were rogues and villains from the first. They had turned prophets, not to speak God's truth, but to make money, to flatter King Ahab, to get themselves a reputation. We do not hear that they were all heathens. Many of them may have believed in the true God. But they were cheats and liars, and so they had given place to the devil, the father of lies: and now he had taken possession of them in spite of themselves, and they lied to Ahab, and told him that he would prosper in the battle at Ramoth-Gilead. It was a dangerous thing for them to say; for if he had been defeated, and returned disappointed, his rage would have most probably fallen on them for deceiving them. And as in those Eastern countries kings do whatever they like without laws or parliaments, Ahab would have most likely put them all to a miserable death on the spot. But however dangerous it might be for them to lie, they could not help lying. A spirit of lies had seized them, and they who began by lying, because it paid them, now could not help doing so whether it paid them or not.

But the good king of Judah, Jehoshaphat, had no faith in these flattering villains. He asked whether there was not another prophet of the Lord to inquire of? Ahab told him that there was one, Micaiah the son of Imlah, but that he hated him, because he only prophesied evil of him. What a thorough picture of a hardened sinner—a man who has become a slave to his own lusts, till he cares nothing for a thing being true, provided only it is pleasant! Thus the wilful sinner, like Ahab, becomes both fool and coward, afraid to look at things as they are; and when God's judgments stare him in the face, the wretched man shuts his eyes tight, and swears that the evil is not there, just because he does not choose to see it.

But the evil was there, ready for Ahab, and it found him. When he forced Micaiah to speak, Micaiah told him the whole truth. He told him a vision, or dream, which he had seen. "Hear thou therefore the word of the Lord: I saw the Lord sitting on His throne, and all the host of heaven standing by Him. And the Lord said, Who shall persuade Ahab, that he may go up and fall at Ramoth-Gilead? And there came forth a spirit, and said, I will go forth, and be a lying spirit in the mouth of all his prophets. And the Lord said, Thou shalt persuade him, and prevail also: go forth, and do so. Now therefore, behold, the Lord hath put a lying spirit in the mouth of all these thy prophets, and the Lord hath spoken evil concerning thee."

What warning could be more awful, and yet more plain? Ahab was told that he was listening to a lie. He had free choice to follow that lie or not, and he did follow it. After having put Micaiah into prison for speaking the truth to him, he went up to Ramoth-Gilead; and yet he felt he was not safe. He had his doubts and his fears. He would not go openly into the battle, but disguised himself, hoping that by this means he should keep himself safe from evil. Fool! God's vengeance could not be stopped by his paltry cunning. In spite of all his disguises, a chance shot struck him down between the joints of his armour. His chariot-driver carried him out of the battle, and "he was stayed up in his chariot against the Syrians, and died at even: and the blood ran out of his wound into the midst of the chariot. And one washed the chariot in the pool of Samaria; and the dogs licked up his blood there," according to the word of the Lord, which He spoke by the mouth of His prophet Elijah, saying, "In the place where dogs licked the blood of Naboth, whom thou slewest, shall dogs lick thy blood, even thine."

And do not fancy, my friends, that because this is a miraculous story of ancient times, it has nothing to do with us. All these things were written for our example. This chapter tells us not merely how Ahab was tempted, but it tells us how *we* are tempted, every one of us, here in England, in these very days. As it was with Ahab, so it is with us. Every wilful sin that we commit we give room to the devil. Every wrong step that we take knowingly, we give a handle to some evil spirit to lead us seven steps further wrong. And yet in every temptation God gives us a fair chance. He is no cruel tyrant who will deliver us over to the devil, to be led helpless and blindfold to our ruin. He did not give Ahab over to him so. He sent a lying spirit to deceive Ahab's prophets, that Ahab might go up and fall at Ramoth-Gilead; but at the very same time, see, he sends a holy and a true man, a man whom Ahab could trust, and did trust at the bottom of his heart, to tell him that the lie was a lie, to warn him of his ruin, so that he might have no excuse for listening to those false prophets—no excuse for following his own pride, his own ambition, to his destruction. So you see, "Let no man say, when he is tempted, I am tempted of God, for God tempteth no man, but every one is tempted when he is led away by his own lust and enticed." Ahab was led away by his own lust; his cowardly love of hearing what was pleasant and flattering to him, rather than what was true—rather than what he knew he deserved; that was what enticed him to listen to Zedekiah and the false prophets, rather than to Micaiah the son of Imlah. *That* is what entices us to sin—the lust of believing what is pleasant to us, what suits our own self-will—what is pleasant to our bodies—pleasant to our purses—pleasant to our pride and self-conceit. Then, when the lying spirit comes and whispers to us, by bad thoughts, by bad books, by bad men, that we shall prosper in our wickedness, does God leave us alone to listen to those evil voices without warning? No! He sends His prophets to us, as He sent Micaiah to Ahab, to tell us that the wages of sin is death—to tell us that those who sow the wind shall reap the whirlwind—to set before us at every turn good or evil, that we may choose between them, and live or die according to our choice. For do not fancy that there are no prophets in our days, unless the gift of the Holy Spirit, which is promised to all who believe, be a dream and a lie. There are prophets nowadays,—yea, I say unto you, and more than prophets. Is not the Bible a prophet? Is not every page in it a prophecy to us, foretelling God's mercies and God's punishments towards men. Is not every holy and wise book, every holy and wise preacher and writer, a prophet, expounding to us God's laws, foretelling to us God's opinions of our deeds, both good and evil? Ay, is not every man a prophet to himself? That "still small voice" in a man's heart, which warns him of what is evil—that feeling which makes him cheerful and free when he has done right, sad and ashamed when he has done wrong—is not that a prophecy in a man's own heart? Truly it is. It is the voice of God within us—it is the Spirit of God striving with our spirits, whether we will hear, or whether we will forbear—setting before us what is righteous, and noble, and pure, and what is manly and God-like—to see whether we will obey that voice, or whether we will obey our own selfish lusts, which tempt us to please ourselves—to pamper ourselves, our greediness, covetousness, ambition, or self-conceit. And again, I say, we have our prophets. Every preacher of righteousness is a prophet. Every good tract is a prophet. That Prayer-book, those Psalms, those Creeds, those Collects, which you take into your mouths every Sunday, what are they but written prophecies, crying unto us with the words of holy men of old, greater than Micaiah, or David, or Elijah, "Hear thou the word of the Lord?" The spirits of those who wrote that Prayer-book—the spirits of just men made perfect, filled with the Spirit of the Lord—they call to us to learn the wisdom which they knew, to avoid the temptations which they conquered, that we may share in the glory in which they shared round the throne of Christ for evermore.

And if you ask me how to try the spirits, how to know whether your own thoughts, whether the sermons which you hear, the books which you read, are speaking to you God's truth, or some lying spirit's falsehood, I can only answer you, "To the law and to the testimony"—to the Bible; if they speak not according to that word, there is no truth in them. But how to understand the Bible? for the fleshly man understands not the things of God. The fleshly man, he who cares only about pleasing himself, he who goes to the Bible full of self-conceit and selfishness, wanting the Bible to tell him only just what he likes to hear, will only find it a sealed book to him, and will very likely wrest the Scriptures to his own destruction. Take up your Bible humbly, praying to God to shew you its meaning, whether it be pleasant to you or not, and then you will find that God will shew you a blessed meaning in it; He will open your eyes, that you may understand the wondrous things of His law; He will shew you how to try the spirit of all you are taught, and to find out whether it comes from God.

SERMON IX.
HELL ON EARTH.

MATTHEW, viii. 29.

"And behold the evil spirits cried out, saying, What have we to do with Thee, Jesus, Thou Son of God? Art Thou come hither to torment us before the time?"

THIS account of the man possessed with devils, and of his language to our Lord, of our Lord's casting the devils out of the poor sufferer, and His allowing them to enter into a herd of swine, is one that is well worth serious thought; and I think a few words on it will follow fitly after my last Sunday's sermon on Ahab and his temptations by evil spirits. In that sermon I shewed you what temper of mind it was which laid a man open to the cunning of evil spirits; I wish now to shew you something of what those evil spirits are. It is very little that we can know about them. We were intended to know very little, just as much as would enable us to guard against them, and no more. The accounts of them in the Scriptures are for our use, not to satisfy our curiosity. But we may find out a great deal about them from this very chapter, from this very story, which is repeated almost word for word in three different Gospels, as if to make us more certain of so curious and important a matter, by having three distinct and independent writers to witness for its truth. I advise all those who have Bibles to look for this story in the 8th chapter of St. Matthew, and follow me as I explain it. [92]

Now, first, we may learn from this account, that evil spirits are real persons. There is a notion got abroad that it is only a figure of speech to talk of evil spirits, that all the Bible means by them are certain bad habits, or bad qualities, or diseases. There are many who will say when they read this story, 'This poor man was only a madman. It was the fashion of the old Jews when a man was mad to say that he was possessed by evil spirits. All they meant was that the man's own spirit was in an evil diseased state, or that his brain and mind were out of order.'

When I hear such language—and it is very common—I cannot help thinking how pleased the devil must be to hear people talk in such a way. How can people help him better than by saying that there is no devil? A thief would be very glad to hear you say, 'There are no such things as thieves; it is all an old superstition, so I may leave my house open at night without danger;' and I believe, my friends, from the very bottom of my heart, that this new-fangled disbelief in evil spirits is put into men's hearts by the evil spirits themselves. As it was once said, 'The devil has tried every plan to catch men's souls, and now, as the last and most cunning trick of all, he is shamming dead.' These may seem homely words, but the homeliest words are very often the deepest. I advise you all to think seriously on them.

But it is impossible surely to read this story without seeing that the Bible considers evil spirits as distinct persons, just as much as each one of us is a person, and that our Lord spoke to them and treated them as persons. "What have *we* to do with Thee, Jesus, Thou Son of God? Art Thou come hither to torment *us* before the time?" And again, "If Thou cast *us* out, suffer us to go into the herd of swine." What can shew more plainly that there were some persons in that poor man, besides himself, his own spirit, his own person? and that *he* knew it, and Jesus knew it too? and that He spoke to these spirits, these persons, who possessed that man, and not to the man himself? No doubt there was a terrible confusion in the poor madman's mind about these evil spirits, who were tormenting him, making him miserable, foul, and savage, in mind and body—a terrible confusion! We find, when Jesus asked him his name, he answers "*Legion*," that is an army, a multitude, "for we are many," he says. Again, one gospel tells us that he says, "What have *I* to do with Thee, Jesus, Thou Son of God?" While in another Gospel we are told that he said, "What have *we* to do with Thee?" He seems not to have been able to distinguish between his own spirit, and these spirits who possessed him. They put the furious and despairing thoughts into his heart; they spoke through his mouth; they made a slave and a puppet of him. But though he could not distinguish between his own soul and the devils who were in it, Christ could and Christ did.

The man says to Him, or rather the devils make the man say to Him, "If Thou cast us out, suffer us to go into the herd of swine, and drive us not out into the deep." What did Christ answer him? Christ did not answer him as our so-called wise men in these days would, 'My good man, this is all a delusion and a fancy of your own, about your having evil spirits in you—more persons than one in you—for you are wrong in saying *we* of yourself. You ought to say "I," as every one else does; and as for spirits going out of you, or going into a herd of swine, or anything else, that is all a superstition and a fancy. There is nothing to come out of you, there is nothing in you except yourself. All the evil in you is your own, the disease of your own brain, and the violent passions of your own heart. Your brain must be cured by medicine, and your violent passions tamed down by care and kindness, and then you will get rid of this foolish notion that you have evil spirits in you, and calling yourself a multitude, as if you had other persons in you besides yourself.'

Any one who spoke in this manner nowadays would be thought very reasonable and very kind. Why did not our Lord speak so to this man, for there was no outward difference between this man's conduct and that of many violent mad people whom we see continually in England? We read, that this man possessed with devils would wear no clothes; that he had extraordinary strength; that he would not keep company with other men, but abode day and night in the tombs, exceeding fierce, crying and cutting himself with stones, trying in blind rage, which he could not explain to himself, to hurt himself and all who came near him. And, above all, he had this notion, that evil spirits had got possession of him. Now every one of these habits and fancies you may see in many raging maniacs at this day.

But did our Lord treat this man as we treat such maniacs in these days? He took the man at his word, and more; the man could not distinguish clearly between himself and the evil spirits, but our Lord did. When the devils besought Him, saying, "If thou cast us out, suffer us to go into the herd of swine," our Lord answers "Go;" and "when they were cast out, they went into the herd of swine; and, behold, the whole herd of swine ran violently down a steep place into the sea, and perished in the waters."

It was as if our Lord had meant to say to the bystanders,—ay and to us, and to all people in all times and in all countries, 'This poor possessed maniac's notion was a true one. There were other persons in him besides himself, tormenting him, body and soul: and, behold, I can drive these out of him and send them into something else, and leave the man uninjured, *himself*, and only himself, again in an instant, without any need of long education to cure him of his bad habits.' It will be but reasonable, then, for us to take this story of the man possessed by devils, as written for our example, as an instance of what *might*, and perhaps *would*, happen to any one of us, were it not for God's mercy.

St. Peter tells us to be sober and watchful, because "the devil goes about as a roaring lion, seeking whom he may devour;" and when we look at the world around, we may surely see that that stands as true now as it did in St. Peter's time. Why, again, did St. James tells us to resist the devil if the devil be not near us to resist? Why did St. Paul take for granted, as he did, that Christian men were, of course, not ignorant of Satan's devices, if it be quite a proof of enlightenment and superior knowledge to be ignorant of his devices,—if any dread, any thought even, about evil spirits, be beneath the attention of reasonable men? My friends, I say fairly, once for all, that that common notion, that there are no men now possessed by evil spirits, and that all those stories of the devil's power over men are only old, worn-out superstitions has come from this, that men do not like to retain God in their knowledge, and therefore, as a necessary consequence, do not like to retain the devil in their knowledge; because they would be very glad to believe in nothing but what they can see, and taste, and handle; and, therefore, the thought of unseen evil spirits, or good spirits either, is a painful thing to them. First, they do not really believe in angels—ministering spirits sent out to minister to the heirs of salvation; then they begin not to believe in evil spirits. The

Bible plainly describes their vast numbers; but these people are wiser than the Bible, and only talk of *one*—of *the* devil, as if there were not, as the text tells us, legions and armies of devils. Then they get rid of that one devil in their real desire to believe in as few spirits as possible. I am afraid many of them have gone on to the next step, and got rid of the one God out of their thoughts and their belief. I said I am afraid, I ought to have said I *know*, that they have done so, and that thousands in this day who began by saying evil spirits only mean certain diseases and bad habits in men, have ended by saying, "God only means certain good habits in man. God is no more a person than the evil spirits are persons."

I warn you of all this, my friends, because if you go to live in large towns, as many of you will, you will hear talk enough of this sort before your hairs are grey, put cleverly and eloquently enough; for, as a wise man said, "The devil does not send fools on his errands." I pray God, that if you ever do hear doctrines of that kind, some of my words may rise in your mind and help to shew to you the evil path down which they lead.

We may believe, then, from the plain words of Scriptures, that there are vast numbers of evil spirits continually tempting men, each of them to some particular sin; to worldliness, for instance, for we read of the spirit of the evil world; to filthiness, for we read of unclean spirits; to falsehood, for we read of lying spirits and a spirit of lies; to pride, for we read of a spirit of pride;—in short, to all sins which a man *can* commit, to all evil passions to which a man can give way. We have a right to believe, from the plain words of Scripture, that these spirits are continually wandering up and down tempting men to sin. That wonderful story of Job's temptation, which you may all read for yourselves in the first chapter of the book of Job, is, I think, proof enough for any one.

But next, and I wish you to pay special attention to this point: We have no right to believe,—we have every right *not* to believe, that these evil spirits can make us sin in the smallest matter against our own wills. The devil cannot put a single sin into us; he can only flatter the sinfulness which is already in us. For, see; this pride, lust, covetousness, falsehood, and so on, to which the Bible tells us they tempt us, have roots already in our nature. Our fallen nature of itself is inclined to pride, to worldliness, and so on. These devils tempt us by putting in our way the occasion to sin, by suggesting to us tempting thoughts and arguments which lead to sin; so the serpent tempted Eve, not by making her ambitious and self-willed, but by using arguments to her which stirred up the ambition and self-will in her: "Ye shall be as gods, knowing good and evil," the devil said to her.

So Satan, the prince of the evil spirits, tempted our Lord. And as the prince of the devils tempted Christ, so do *his* servants tempt *us*, Christ's servants. Our tempers, our longings, our fancies, are not evil spirits; they are, as old divines well describe them, like greedy and foolish fish, who rise at the baits which evil spirits hold out to us. If we resist those baits—if we put ourselves under God's protection—if we claim strength from Him who conquered the devil and all His temptations, then we shall be able to turn our wills away from those tempting baits, and to resign our wills into our Father's hand, and He will take care of them, and strengthen them with His will; and we shall find out that if we resist the devil, he will flee from us. But if we yield to temptations whenever they come in our way, we shall find ourselves less and less able to resist them, for we shall learn to hate the evil spirits less and less; I mean we shall shrink less from the evil thoughts they hold out to us. We shall give place to the devil, as the Scripture tells us we shall; for instance, by indulging in habitual passionate tempers, or rooted spite and malice, letting the sun go down upon our wrath: and so a man may become more and more the slave of his own nature, of his own lusts and passions, and therefore of the devils, who are continually pampering and maddening those lusts and passions, till a man may end in *complete possession*; not in common madness, which may be mere disease, but as a savage and a raging maniac, such as, thank God, are rare in Christian countries, though they were common among our own forefathers before they were converted to Christianity,—men like the demoniac of whom the text speaks, tormented by devils, given up to blind rage and malice against himself and all around, to lust and blasphemy, to confusion of mind and misery of body, God's image gone, and the image of the devil, the destroyer and the corrupter, arisen in its place. Few men can arrive at this pitch of wretchedness in a civilised country. It would not answer the evil spirit's purpose to let them do so. It suits *his* spirits best in such a land as this to walk about dressed up as angels of light. Few men in England would be fools enough to indulge the gross and fierce part of their nature till they became mere savages, like the demoniac whom Christ cured; so it is to respectable vices that the devil mostly tempts us,—to covetousness, to party spirit, to a hard heart and a narrow mind; to cruelty, that shall clothe itself under the name of law; to filthiness, which excuses itself by saying, "It is a man's nature, he cannot help it;" to idleness, which excuses itself on the score of wealth; to meanness and unfairness in trade, and in political and religious disputes—these are the devils which haunt us Englishmen—sleek, prim, respectable fiends enough; and, truly, *their* name is Legion! And the man who gives himself up to them, though he may not become a raving savage, is just as truly possessed by devils, to his own misery and ruin, that he may sow the wind and reap the whirlwind; that though men may speak well of him, and posterity praise his saying, and speak good of the covetous whom God abhorreth, yet he may go for ever unto his own, to the evil spirits to whom his own wicked will gave him up for a prey. I beseech you, my friends, consider my words; they are not mine, but the Bible's. Think of them with fear;—and yet with confidence, for we are baptised into the name of Him who conquered all devils; you may claim a share in that Spirit which is opposite to all evil spirits,—whose presence makes the agony and misery of evil spirits, and drives them out as water drives out fire. If He is on your side, why should you be afraid of any spirit? Greater is He that is in you than he that is against you; and He, Christ Himself, is with every man, every child, who struggles, however blindly and weakly, against temptation. When temptation comes, when evil looks pleasant, and arguments rise up in your mind, that seem to make it look right and reasonable, as well as pleasant, *then*, out of the very depths of your hearts, cry after Him who died for you. Say to yourselves, 'How can I do this thing, and offend against Him who bought me with His blood?' Say to Him, 'I am weak, I am confused; I do not see right from wrong; I cannot find my way; I cannot answer the devil; I cannot conquer these cunning thoughts; I know in the bottom of my heart that they are wrong, mere temptations, and yet they look so reasonable. Blessed Saviour, *Thou* must shew me where they are wrong. Thou didst answer the devil Thyself out of God's Word, put into *my* mind some answer out of God's Word to these temptations; or, at least, give me spirit to toss them off—strength of will to thrust the whole temptation out of my head, and say, I will parley no longer with the devil; I will put the whole matter out of my head for a time. I don't know whether it is right or wrong for me to do this particular thing, but there are twenty other things which I *do* know are right. I'll go and do *them*, and let this wait awhile.'

Believe me, my friends, you *can* do this—you can resist these evil spirits which tempt us all; else why did our Lord bid us pray, "Lead us not into temptation, but deliver us from evil?" Why? Because our Father in heaven, if we ask Him, will *not* lead us *into* temptation, but *through* it safe. Tempted we *must* be, else we should not be men; but here is our comfort and our strength—that we have a King in heaven, who has fought out and conquered all temptations, and a Father in heaven, who has promised that He will not suffer us to be tempted above that we are able, but will, with the temptation, make a way to escape, that we may be able to bear it.

Again, I say, draw near to God, and He will draw near to you. Resist the devil, and he will flee from you.

SERMON X.
NOAH'S JUSTICE.

GENESIS, vi. 9.

"Noah was a just man and perfect in his generations, and Noah walked with God."

I INTEND, my friends, according as God shall help me, to preach to you, between this time and Christmas, a few sermons on some of the saints and worthies of the Old Testament; and I will begin this day with Noah.

Now you must bear in mind that the histories of these ancient men were, as St. Paul says, written for our example. If these men in old times had been different from us, they would not be examples to us; but they were like us—men of like passions, says St. James, as ourselves; they had each of them in them a corrupt *nature*, which was continually ready to drag them down, and make beasts of them, and make them slaves to their own lusts—slaves to eating and drinking, and covetousness, and cowardice, and laziness, and love for the things which they could see and handle—just such a nature, in short, as we have. And they had also a spirit in each of them which was longing to be free, and strong, and holy, and wise—such a spirit as we have. And to them, just as to us, God was revealing himself; God was saying to their consciences, as He does to ours, 'This is right, that is wrong; do this, and be free and clear-hearted; do that, and be dark and discontented, and afraid of thy own thoughts.' And they too, like us, had to live by faith, by continual belief that they owed a *duty* to the great God whom they could not see, by continual belief that He loved them, and was guiding and leading them through every thing which happened, good or ill.

This is faith in God, by which alone we, or any man, can live worthily,—by which these old heroes lived. We read, in the twelfth chapter of Hebrews, that it was by faith these elders obtained a good report; and the whole history of the Old-Testament saints is the history of God speaking to the hearts of one man after another, teaching them each more and more about Himself, and the history also of these men listening to the voice of God in their hearts, and *believing* that voice, and acting faithfully upon it, into whatever strange circumstances or deeds it might lead them. "By faith," we read in this same chapter,—"by faith Noah, being warned of God, prepared an ark to the saving of his house, and became heir of the righteousness which is by faith."

Now, to understand this last sentence, you must remember that Noah was not under the law of Moses. St. Paul has a whole chapter (the third chapter of Galatians) to shew that these old saints had nothing to do with Moses' law any more than we have, that it was given to the Jews many hundred years afterwards. So these histories of the Old-Testament saints are, in fact, histories of men who conquered by faith—histories of the power which faith in God has to conquer temptation, and doubt, and false appearances, and fear, and danger, and all which besets us and keeps us down from being free and holy, and children of the day, walking cheerfully forward on our heavenward road in the light of our Father's loving smile.

Noah, we read, "was a just man, and perfect in his generations;" and why? Because he was a faithful man—faithful to God, as it is written, "The just shall live by his faith;" not by trusting in what he does himself, in his own works or deservings, but trusting in God who made him, believing that God is perfectly righteous, perfectly wise, perfectly loving; and that, because He is perfectly loving, He will accept and save sinful man when He sees in sinful man the earnest wish to be His faithful, obedient servant, and to give himself up to the rule and guidance of God. This, then, was Noah's justice in God's sight, as it was Abraham's. They believed God, and so became heirs of the righteousness which is by faith; not their own righteousness, not growing out of their own character, but given them by God, who puts His righteous Spirit into those who trust in Him.

But, moreover, we read that Noah "was perfect in his generations;" that is, he was perfect in all the relations and duties of life,—a good son, a good husband, a good father: these were the fruits of his faith. He believed that the unseen God had given him these ties, had given him his parents, his children, and that to love them was to love God, to do his duty to them was to do his duty to God. This was part of his walking with God, continually under his great Taskmaster's eye,—walking about his daily business with the belief that a great loving Father was above him, whatever he did; ready to strengthen, and guide, and bless him if he did well, ready to avenge Himself on him if he did ill. These were the fruits of Noah's faith.

But you may think this nothing very wonderful. Many a man in England does this every day, and yet no one ever hears of him; he attends to all his family ties, doing justly, loving mercy, and walking humbly with God, like one who knows he is redeemed by Christ's blood; he lives, he dies, he is buried, and out of his own parish his name is never known; while Noah has earned for himself a worldwide fame; for four thousand years his name has been spreading over the whole earth as one of the greatest men who ever lived. Mighty nations have worshipped Noah as a God; many heathen nations worship him under strange and confused names and traditions to this day; and the wisest and holiest men among Christians now reverence Noah, write of him, preach on him, thank God for him, look up to him as, next to Abraham, their greatest example in the Old Testament.

Well, my friends, to understand what made Noah so great, we must understand in what times Noah lived. "The wickedness of men was great in the earth in those days, and every imagination of the thoughts of their heart was only evil continually, and the earth was filled with violence through them." And we must remember that the wickedness of men before the flood was not outwardly like wickedness now; it was not petty, mean, contemptible wickedness of silly and stupid men, such as could be despised and laughed down; it was like the wickedness of fallen angels. Men were then strong and beautiful, cunning and active, to a degree of which we can form no conception. Their enormous length of life (six, seven, and eight hundred years commonly) must have given them an experience and daring far beyond any man in these days. Their bodily size and strength were in many cases enormous. We read that "there were giants in the earth in those days; and also after that, when the sons of God came in unto the daughters of men, and they bare children to them, the same became mighty men which were of old, men of renown." Their powers of invention seem to have been proportionably great. We read, in the fourth chapter of Genesis, how, within a few years after Adam was driven out of Paradise, they had learned to build cities, to tame the wild beasts, and live upon their milk and flesh; that they had invented all sorts of music and musical instruments; that they had discovered the art of working in metals. We read among them of Tubal-Cain, an instructor of every workman in brass and iron; and the old traditions in the East, where these men dwelt, are full of strange and awful tales of their power.

Again, we must remember that there was no law in Noah's days before the flood, no Bible to guide them, no constitutions and acts of parliament to bind men in the beaten track by the awful majesty of law, whether they will or no, as we have.

This is the picture which the Bible gives us of the old world before the flood—a world of men mighty in body and mind, fierce and busy, conquering the world round them, in continual war and turmoil; with all the wild passions of youth, and yet all the cunning and experience of enormous old age; with the strength and the courage of young men to carry out the iniquity of old ones; every one guided only by self-will, having cast off God and conscience, and doing every man that which was right in the sight of his own eyes. And amidst all this, while men, as wise, as old, as strong, as great as himself, whirled away round him in this raging sea of sin, Noah was stedfast; he, at least, knew his way,—"he walked with God, a just man, and perfect in his generations."

To Noah, living in such a world as this, among temptation, and violence, and insult, no doubt, there came this command from God: "The end of all flesh is come before me, for the earth is filled with violence through them, and I will destroy them with the earth. And behold I, even I, do bring a flood of waters upon the earth, to destroy all flesh wherein is the breath of life; but with thee will I establish my covenant, and thou shalt make thee an ark of wood after the fashion which I tell thee; and thou shalt come into the ark, thou and thy family, and of every living thing, two of every sort, male and female, shalt thou bring into the ark, and keep them alive with thee; and take thou of all food that is eaten into the ark, for thee and for them." What a message, my friends! If we wish to see a little of the greatness of Noah's faith, conceive such a message coming from God to one of us! Should we believe it—much less act upon it? But *Noah* believed God, says the Scripture; and "according as God commanded him, so did he." Now, in whatever way this command came from God to Noah, it is equally wonderful. Some of you, perhaps, will say in your hearts, 'No! when God spoke to him, how could he help obeying Him?' But, my friends, ask yourselves seriously,—for, believe me, it is a most important question for the soul and inner life of you and me, and every man—how did Noah know that it was God who spoke to him? It is easy to say God appeared to him; but no man hath seen God at any time. It is easy, again, to say that an angel appeared to him, or that God appeared to him in the form of a man; but still the same question is left to be answered, how did he know that this appearance came from God, and that its words were true? Why should not Noah have said, 'This was an evil spirit which appeared to me, trying to frighten and ruin me, and stir up all my neighbours to mock me, perhaps to murder me?' Or, again; suppose that you or I saw some glorious apparition this day, which told us on such and such a day such and such a town will be destroyed, what should *we* think of it? Should we not say, I must have been dreaming—I must have been ill, and so my brain and eyes must have been disordered, and treat the whole thing as a mere fancy of ill-health; now why did not Noah do the same?

Why do I say this? To shew you, my friends, that it is not apparitions and visions which can make a man believe. As it is written, "If they believe not Moses and the prophets, neither will they believe though one rose from the dead." No; a man must have faith in his heart already. A man must first be accustomed to discern right from wrong—to listen to and to obey the voice of God within him; *that* word of God of which it is said, "the word is nigh thee, in thy heart, and in thy mind," before he can hear God's word from without; else he will only explain away miracles, and call visions and apparitions sick men's dreams.

But there was something yet more wonderful and divine in Noah's faith,—I mean his patience. He knew that a flood was to come—he set to work in faith to build his ark—and that ark was in building for one hundred and twenty years,—one hundred and twenty years! It seems at first past all belief. For all that time he built; and all the while the world went on just as usual; and, before he had finished, old men had died, and children grown into years; and great cities had sprung up perhaps where there was not a cottage before; and trees which were but a yard high when that ark was begun had grown into mighty forest-timber; and men had multiplied and spread, and yet Noah built and built on stedfastly, believing that what God had said would surely one day or other come to pass. For one hundred and twenty years he saw the world go on as usual, and yet he never forgot that it was a doomed world. He endured the laughter and mockery of all his neighbours, and every fresh child who was born grew up to laugh at the foolish old man who had been toiling for a hundred years past on his mad scheme, as they thought it; and yet Noah never lost faith, and he never lost *love* either—for all those years, we read, he preached righteousness to the very men who mocked him, and preached in vain—one hundred and twenty years he warned those sinners of God's wrath, of righteousness and judgment to come, and no man listened to him! That, I believe, must have been, after all, the hardest of all his trials.

And, doubtless, Noah had his inward temptation many a time; no doubt he was ready now and then to believe God's message all a dream—to laugh at himself for his fears of a flood which seemed never coming, but in his heart was "the still small voice" of God, warning him that God was not a man that he should lie, or repent, or deceive those who walked faithfully with him; and around him he saw men growing and growing in iniquity, filling up the cup of their own damnation; and he said to himself, 'Verily there is a God who judgeth the earth—for all this a reckoning day will surely come;' and he worked stedfastly on, and the ark was finished. And then at last there came a second call from God, "Come thou and all thy house into the ark, for thee have I seen righteous before me in this generation. Yet seven days, and I will cause it to rain upon the earth, and every living substance that I have made will I destroy from off the earth." And Noah entered into the ark, and seven days he waited; and louder than ever laughed the scoffers round him, at the old man and his family shut into his ark safe on dry land, while day and night went on as quietly as ever, and the world ran its usual round; for seven days more their mad game lasted—they ate, they drank, they married, they gave in marriage, they planted, they builded; and on the seventh day it came—the rain fell day after day, and week after week—and the windows of heaven were opened, and the fountains of the great deep were broken up, and the flood arose, and swept them all away!

SERMON XI.
THE NOACHIC COVENANT.

Gen. ix. 8, 9.

"And God spake unto Noah, and his sons with him, saying, And I, behold, I establish my covenant with you, and with your seed after you."

In my last sermon on Noah I spoke of the flood and of Noah's faith before the flood; I now go on to speak of the covenant which God made with Noah after the flood. Now, Noah stood on that newly-dried earth as the head of mankind; he and his family, in all eight souls, saved by God's mercy from the general ruin, were the only human beings left alive, and had laid on them the wonderful and glorious duty of renewing the race of man, and replenishing the vast world around them. From that little knot of human beings were to spring all the nations of the earth.

And because this calling and destiny of theirs was a great and all-important one—because so much of the happiness or misery of the new race of mankind depended on the teaching which they would get from their forefathers, the sons of Noah, therefore God thought fit to make with Noah and his sons a solemn covenant, as soon as they came out of the ark.

Let us solemnly consider this covenant, for it stands good now as much as ever. God made it "with Noah, and his seed after him," for perpetual generations. And *we* are the seed of Noah; every man, woman, and child of us here were in the loins of Noah when the great absolute God gave him that pledge and promise. We must earnestly consider that covenant, for in it lies the very ground and meaning of man's life and business on this earth.

"And God blessed Noah and his sons, and said unto them, Be fruitful and multiply, and replenish the earth; and the fear of you and the dread of you shall be upon every living creature. Into your hand they are delivered. Every moving thing that liveth shall be meat for you, even as the green herb have I given you all things. But flesh with the life thereof, which is the blood thereof shall ye not eat. And surely your blood of your lives will I require; at the hand of every beast will I require it, and at the hand of men; at the hand of every man's brother will I require the life of man. Whoso sheddeth man's blood, by man shall his blood be shed; for in the image of God made He man."

Now, to understand this covenant, consider what thoughts would have been likely to grow up in the mind of Noah's children after the flood. Would they not have been something of this kind: 'God does not love men; He has drowned all but us, and we are men of like passions with the world who perished, may we not expect the like ruin at any moment? Then what use to plough and sow, and build and plant, and work for those who shall come after us?' 'Let us eat and drink, for to-morrow we die.'

And again, they would have been ready to say, 'This God, whom our forefather Noah said sent floods, we cannot see Him; but the floods themselves we can see. All these clouds and tempests, lightning, sun, and stars, are we *stronger* than them? No! They may crush us, drown us, strike us dead at any moment. They seem, too, to go by certain wonderful rules and laws; perhaps they have a will and understanding in them. Instead of praying to a God whom we never saw, why not pray to the thunderclouds not to strike us dead, and to the seas and rivers not to sweep us away? For this great, wonderful, awful world in which we are, however beautiful may be its flowers, and its fruits, and its sunshine, there is no trusting it; we are sitting upon a painted sepulchre, a beautiful monster, a gulf of flood and fire, which may burst up any moment, and sweep us away, as it did our forefathers.'

Again, Noah's children would have begun to say, 'These beasts here round us, they are so many of them larger than us, stronger than us, able to tear us to atoms, eat us up as they would eat a lamb. They are self-sufficient, too; they want no clothes, nor houses, nor fire, like us poor, weak, naked, soft human creatures. They can run faster than we, see farther than we; their scent, too, what a wonderful, mysterious power that is, like a miracle to us! And, besides all their cunning ways of getting food and building nests, they never do *wrong*; they never do horrible things contrary to their nature; they all abide as God has made them, obeying the law of their kind. Are not these beasts, then, much wiser and better than we? We will honour them, and pray to them not to devour us—to make us cunning and powerful as they are themselves. And if they are no better than us, surely they are no worse than us. After all, what difference is there between a man and a beast? The flood which drowned the beasts drowned the men too. A beast is flesh and blood, what more is a man? If you kill him, he dies, just as a beast dies; and why should not a man's carcase be just as good to eat as a beast's, and better?' And so there would have been a free opening at once into all the horrors of cannibalism!

Again, Noah's descendants would have said, 'Our forefathers offered sacrifices to the unseen God, as a sign that all they had belonged to Him, and that they had forfeited their own souls by sin, and were therefore ready to give up the most precious things they had—their cattle, as a sign that they owed all to that very God whom they had offended. But are not human creatures much more precious than cattle? Will it not be a much greater sign of repentance and willingness to give up all to God if we offer Him the best things which we have—human creatures? If we kill and sacrifice to Him our most beautiful and innocent things—little children—noble young men—beautiful young girls?'

My friends, these are very strange and shocking thoughts, but they have been in the hearts and minds of all nations. The heathens do such things now. Our own forefathers used to do such things once; they were tempted to worship the sun and the moon, and the rivers, and the thunder, and to look with superstitious terror at the bears, and the wolves, and the snakes, round them, and to kill their young children and maidens, and offer them up as sacrifices to the dark powers of this world, which they thought were ready to swallow them up. And God is my witness, my friends, when one goes through some parts of England now, and sees the mine-children and factory-children, and all the sin and misery, and the people wearying themselves in the fire for very vanity, we seem not to be so very far from the same dark superstition now, though we may call it by a different name. England has been sacrificing her sons and her daughters to the devil of covetousness of late years, just as much as our forefathers offered theirs to the devil of selfish and cowardly superstition.

But see, now, how this covenant which God made with Noah was intended just to remedy every one of those temptations which I just mentioned, into which Noah's children's children would have been certain to fall, and into which so many of them did fall. They might have become reckless, I said, from fear of a flood at any moment. God promises them—and confirms it with the sign of the rainbow—never again to destroy the earth by water. They would have been likely to take to praying to the rain and the thunder, the sun and the stars; God declares in this covenant that it is *He* alone who sends the rain and thunder, that He brings the clouds over the earth, that He rules the great, awful world; that men are to look up and believe in God as a loving and thinking *person*, who has a will of His own, and that a faithful, and true, and loving, and merciful will; that their lives and safety depend not on blind chance, or the stern necessity of certain laws of nature, but on the covenant of an almighty and all-loving person.

Again, I said, that Noah's sons would have been ready to fear, and, at last, to worship the dumb beasts; God's covenant says, "No; these beasts are not your equals—they are your slaves—you may freely kill them for your food; the fear of you shall be upon them. The huge elephant and the swift horse shall become your obedient servants; the lion and the tiger shall tremble and flee before you. Only claim your rights as men; believe that the invisible God who made the earth is your strength and your protector, and that He to whom the earth belongs has made you lords of the earth and all that therein is. But," said God's covenant to Noah's sons, "you did not *make* these beasts—you did not give them life, therefore I forbid you to eat their blood wherein their life lies; that you may never forget that all the power you have over these beasts was given you by God, who made and preserves that wonderful, mysterious, holy thing called life, which you can never imitate." Again, I said, that Noah's children, having been accustomed to the violence and bloodshed on the earth before the flood, might hold man's life cheap; that, having seen in the flood men perish just like the beasts around them, they might have begun to think that man's life was not more precious than the beasts'. They might have all gone on at last, as some of them did, to those horrors of cannibalism and human sacrifice of which I just now spoke. Now, here, again comes in God's covenant, "Surely the blood of your lives will I require. At the hand of every beast will I require it, and at the hand of every man's brother will I require it. Whoso sheddeth man's blood by man shall his blood be shed, for in the image of God made He man." This, then, is the covenant which God made with Noah for perpetual generations, and therefore with us, the children of Noah. In this covenant you see certain truths come out into light; some, of which you read nothing before in the Bible, and other truths which, though they were given to Adam, yet had been utterly lost sight of before the flood. This has been God's method, we find from the Bible, ever since the creation,—to lead man step by step up into more and more light, up to this very day, and to make each sin and each madness of men an occasion for revealing to Him more and more of truth and of the living God. And so each and every chapter in the Bible is built upon all that has gone before it; and he that neglects to understand what has gone before will never come to the understanding of what follows after. Why do I say this? Because men are continually picking out those scraps of the Bible which suit their own fancy, and pinning their whole faith on them, and trying to make them serve to explain every thing in heaven and earth; whereas no man can understand the Epistles unless he first understand the Gospels. No man will understand the New Testament unless he first understands the pith and marrow of the Old. No man will understand the Psalms and the Prophets unless he first understands the first ten chapters of Genesis; and, lastly, no one will ever understand any thing about the Bible at all, who, instead of taking it simply as it is written, is always trying to twist it into proofs of his own favourite doctrines, and make Abraham a high Calvinist, or Noah a member of the Church of England. Why do I say this? To make you all think seriously that this covenant on which I have been preaching is your covenant; that as sure as the rainbow stands in heaven, as sure as you and I are sprung out of the loins of Noah, so surely this covenant which binds us is part of our Christian covenant, and woe to us if we break it!

This covenant tells us that we are made in God's likeness, and, therefore, that all sin is unworthy of us and unnatural to us. It tells us that God means us bravely and industriously to subdue the earth and the living things upon it; that we are to be the masters of the pleasant things about us, and not their slaves, as sots and idlers are; that we are stewards and tenants of this world for the great God who made it, to whom we are to look up in confidence for help and protection. It tells us that our family relationships, the blessed duties of a husband and a father, are sacred things; that God has created them, that the great God of heaven Himself respects them, that the covenant which He makes with the father He makes with the children; that He commands marriage, and that He blesses it with fruitfulness; that it is He who has told us "Be fruitful and multiply, and replenish the earth;" that the tie of brotherhood is His making also; that *He* will require the blood of the murdered man *at his brother's hand*; that a man's brothers, his nearest relations, are bound to protect and right him if he is injured; so that we all are to be, in the deepest sense of the word, what Cain refused to be, our *brothers' keepers*, and each member of a family is more or less answerable for the welfare and safety of all his relations. Herein lies the ground of all religion and of all society—in the covenant which God made with Noah; and just as it is in vain for a man to pretend to be a scholar when he does not even know his letters, so it is mockery for a man to pretend to be a converted Christian man who knows not even so much as was commanded to Noah and his sons. He who has not learnt to love, honour, and succour his own family—he who has not learnt to work in honest and manful industry—he who has not learnt to look beyond this earth, and its chance, and its customs, and its glittering outside, and see and trust in a great, wise, loving God, by whose will every tree grows and every shower falls, what is Christianity to him? He has to learn the first principles which were delivered to Noah, and which not even the heathen and the savage have utterly forgotten.

SERMON XII.
ABRAHAM'S FAITH.

HEBREWS, xi. 9, 10.

"By faith Abraham sojourned in the land of promise as in a strange country, dwelling in tabernacles with Isaac and Jacob, the heirs with him of the same promise. For he looked for a city, which hath foundations, whose builder and maker is God."

IN the last sermon which I preached in this church, I said that the Bible is the history of God's ways with mankind, how He has schooled and brought them up until the coming of Christ; that if we read the Bible histories, one after another, in the same order in which God has put them in the Bible, we shall see that they are all regular steps in a line, that each fresh story depends on the story which went before it; and yet, in each fresh history, we shall find God telling men something new—something which they did not know before. And that so the whole Bible, from beginning to end, is one glorious, methodic, and organic tree of life, every part growing out of the others and depending on the others, from the root—that foundation, other than which no man can lay, which is Christ, revealing Himself, though not by name, in that wonderful first chapter of Genesis,—up to the *fruit*, which is the kingdom of Christ, and Gospel of Christ, and the salvation in which we here now stand. I told you that the lesson which God has been teaching men in all ages is faith in God—that the saints of old were just the men who learnt this lesson of faith. Now this, as we all know, was the secret of Abraham's greatness, that he had faith in God to leave his own country at God's bidding, and become a stranger and a pilgrim on the earth, wandering on in full trust that God would give him another country instead of that which he had left— "a city which hath foundations, whose builder and maker is God." This was what Abraham looked for. Something of what it means we shall see presently.

You remember the story of the tower of Babel? How certain of Noah's family forgot the covenant which God had made with Noah, forgot that God had commanded them to go forth in every direction and fill the earth with human beings, solemnly promising to protect and bless them, and took on themselves to do the very opposite—set up a kingdom of their own fashion, and herded together for selfish safety, instead of going forth to all the quarters of the world in a natural way, according to their families, in their tribes, after their nations, as the eleventh chapter of Genesis says they ought to have done. "Let us build us a city and a tower, and make us a name, lest," they said, "we be scattered abroad over the face of the whole world." Here was one act of disobedience to God's order. But besides this they had fallen into a slavish dread of the powers of nature—they were afraid of another flood. They set to to build a tower, on which they might worship the sun and stars, and the host of heaven, and pray to them to send no more floods and tempests. They thus fell into a slavish fear of the powers of nature, as well as into a selfish and artificial civilisation. In short, they utterly broke the covenant which God had made with Noah. But by miraculously confounding their language, God drove them forth over the face of the whole earth, and so forced them to do that which they ought to have done willingly at first.

Now, we must remember that all this happened in the very country in which Abraham lived. He must have heard of it all—for aught we know he had seen the tower of Babel. So that, for good or for evil, the whole Babel event must have produced a strong effect on the mind of a thoughtful man like Abraham, and raised many strange questionings in his heart, which God alone could answer for him, *or for us*. Now, what did God mean to teach Abraham by calling him out of his country, and telling him, "I will make of thee a great nation?" I think He meant to shew him, for one thing, that that Babel plan of society was utterly absurd and accursed, certain to come to naught, and so to lead him on to hope for a city which had foundations, and to see that *its* builder and maker must be, not the selfishness or the ambition of men, but the will, and the wisdom, and providence of God.

Let us see how God led Abraham on to understand this—to look for a city which had foundations; in short, to understand what a State and a nation means and ought to be. First, God taught him that he was not to cling coward-like to the place where he was born, but to go out boldly to colonise and subdue the earth, for the great God of heaven would protect and guide him. "Get thee out of thy country and from thy father's house unto a land which I will shew thee. And I will bless them that bless thee, and curse them that curse thee." Again; God taught him what a nation was: "*I* will make of thee a great nation." As much as to say, 'Never fancy, as those fools at Babel did, that a nation only means a great crowd of people—never fancy that men can make themselves into a nation just by feeding altogether, and breeding altogether, and fighting altogether, as the herds of wild cattle and sheep do, while there is no real union between them.' For what brought those Babel men together? Just what keeps a herd of cattle together—selfishness and fear. Each man thought he would be *safer*, forsooth, in company. Each man thought that if he was in company, he could use his neighbours' wits as well as his own, and have the benefit of his neighbours' strength as well as his own. And that is all true enough; but that does not make a nation. Selfishness can join nothing; it may join a set of men for a time, each for his own ends, just as a joint-stock company is made up; but it will soon split them up again. Each man, in a merely selfish community, will begin, after a time, to play on his own account as well as work on his own account—to oppress and overreach for his own ends as well as to be honest and benevolent for his own ends, for he will find ill-doing far easier, and more natural, in one sense, and a plan that brings in quicker profits, than well-doing; and so this godless, loveless, every-man-for-himself nation, or sham nation rather, this joint-stock company, in which fools expect that universal selfishness will do the work of universal benevolence, will quarrel and break up, crumble to dust again, as Babel did. "But," says God to Abraham, "I will make of thee a great nation. I make nations, and not they themselves." So it is, my friends: this is the lesson which God taught Abraham, the lesson which we English must learn nowadays over again, or smart for it bitterly—that God makes nations. He is King of kings; "by Him kings reign and princes decree judgment." He judges all nations: He nurtureth the nations. This is throughout the teaching of the Psalms. "It is He that hath made us, and not we ourselves; we are His people, and the sheep of His pasture;" for this I take to be the true bearing of that glorious national hymn the 100th Psalm, and not merely the old truism that men did not create themselves, when it exhorts *all* nations to praise God because it is He that hath made them nations, and not they themselves. The Psalms set forth the Son of God as the King of all nations. In Him, my friends,—in Him all the nations of the earth are truly blessed.

He the Saviour of a few individual souls only? God forbid! To Him *all power* is given in heaven and earth; by Him were all things created, whether in heaven or earth, visible and invisible, whether they be thrones or dominions, or principalities or powers;—all national life, all forms of government, whether hero-despotisms, republics, or monarchies, aristocracies of birth, or of wealth, or of talent,—all were created by Him and for Him, and He is before all things, and by Him all things *consist* and hold together. Every thing or institution on earth which has systematic and organic life in it—by *Him* it consists—by Him, the Life and the Light who lighteneth every man that cometh into the world. From Him come law, and order, and spiritual energy, and loving fellow-feeling, and patriotism, the spirit of wisdom, and understanding, and prudence—all, in short, by which a nation consists and holds together. It is not constitutions, and acts of parliament, and social contracts, and rights of the people, and rights of kings, and so on, which make us a nation. These are but the effects, and not the consequences, of the national life. *That* is the one spirit which is shed abroad upon a country, whose builder and maker is God, and which comes down from above—comes down from Christ the King of kings, who has given each nation its peculiar work on this earth, its peculiar circumstances and history to mould and educate it for its work, and its peculiar spirit and national character, wherewith to fulfil the destiny which Christ has appointed for it.

Believe me, my friends, it takes long years, too, and much training from God and from Christ, the King of kings, to make a nation. Everything which is most precious and great is also most slow in growing, and so is a nation. The Scripture compares it everywhere to a tree; and as the tree grows, a people must grow, from small beginnings, perhaps from a single family, increasing on, according to the fixed laws of God's world, for years and hundreds of years, till it becomes a mighty nation, with one Lord, one faith, one work, one Spirit.

But again; God said to Abraham, when He had led him into this far country, "Unto thy seed will *I give this land*." This was a great and a new lesson for Abraham, that the earth belonged to that same great invisible God who had promised to guide and protect him, and make him into a nation—that this same God gave the earth to whomsoever He would, and allotted to each people their proper portion of it. "He (said St. Paul on the Areopagus) hath determined the times before appointed for all nations, and the bounds of their habitation, that they may seek after the Lord and find Him." Ah! this must have been a strange and a new feeling to Abraham; but, stranger still, though God had given him this land, he was not to take possession of a single foot of it; the land was already in the hands of a different nation, the people of Canaan; and Abraham was to go wandering about a sojourner, as the text says, in this very land of promise which God had given him, without ever taking possession of his own, simply because it belonged to others already. How this must have taught Abraham that the rights of property were sacred things—things appointed by God; that it was an awful and a heinous sin to make wanton war on other people, to drive them out and take possession of their land; that it was not mere force or mere fancy which gave men a right to a country, but the providence of Almighty God! Now Abraham needed this warning, for the men of Babel seem from the first to have gone on the plan of driving out and conquering the tribes round them. They seem to have set up their city partly from ambition. "Let us make us a name," they said, meaning, 'Let us make ourselves famous and terrible to all the people around us, that we may subdue them.' And we read of Nimrod, who was their first king and the founder of Babel, that he was a mighty hunter before the Lord, that is, as most learned men explain it, a mighty conqueror and tyrant in defiance of God and His laws, as the poet says of him,

> "A mighty hunter, and his game was man."

The Jews, indeed, have an old tradition that Nimrod cast Abraham into a fiery furnace for refusing to worship the host of heaven with him. The story is very likely untrue, but still it is of use in shewing what sort of reputation Nimrod left behind him in his own part of the world. We may thus see that Abraham would need warning against these habits of violence, tyranny, and plunder, into which the men of Babel and other tribes were falling. And this was what God meant to teach him by keeping him a stranger and a pilgrim in the very land which God had promised to him for his own. Thus Abraham learnt respect for the rights and properties of his neighbours; thus he learnt to look up in faith to God, not only as his patron and protector, but as the lord and absolute owner of the soil on which he stood.

Now in the 14th chapter of Genesis there is an account of Abraham's being called on to put in practice what he had learnt, and, by doing so, learning a fresh lesson. We read of four kings making war against five kings, against Chedorlaomer, king of Elam or Persia, who had been following the ways of Nimrod and the men of Babel, and conquering these foreign kings and making them serve him. We read of Chedorlaomer and four other kings coming down and wantonly ravaging and destroying other countries, besides the five kings who had rebelled against them, and at last carrying off captive the people of Sodom and Gomorrah, and Lot, Abraham's nephew. We read then how Abraham armed his trained servants, born in his own house, three hundred and eighteen men, and pursued after these tyrants and plunderers, and with his small force completely overthrew that great army. Now that was a sign and a lesson to Abraham, as much as to say, 'See the fruits of having the great God of heaven and earth for your protector and your guide,—see the fruits of having men round you, not hirelings, keeping in your company just to see what they can get by it, but born in your own house, who love and trust you, whom you can love and trust,—see how the favour of God, and reverence for those family ties and duties which He has appointed, make you and your little band of faithful men superior to these great mobs of selfish, godless, unjust robbers,—see how hundreds of these slaves ran away before one man, who feels that he is a member of a family, and has a just cause for fighting, and that God and his brethren are with him.'

Here, you see, was another hint to Abraham of what it was and who it was that made a great nation.

And now some of you may say, 'This is a strange sermon. You have as yet said nothing of Christ, nothing of the Holy Spirit, nothing of grace, redemption, sanctification. What kind of sermon is this?'

My friends, do not be too sure that I have not been preaching Christ to you, and Christ's Spirit to you, and Christ's redemption too, most truly in this sermon, although I have mentioned none of them by name. There are times for ornamenting the house, there are times for repairing the wall, there are times, too, for thoroughly examining the foundation, because, if that be not sound, it is little matter what fine work is built up upon it; and there are times when, as David says, the foundations of the earth are out of course, when men have forgotten sadly the very first principles of society and religion.

And, surely, men are doing so in these days; men are forgetting that other foundation can no man lay save that which *is* laid, which is Christ; they laugh at the thought of a city, that is, a state and form of government, "not made with hands, eternal in the heavens;" they have forgotten that St. Paul tells them in the Hebrews that we *have* "a city which hath foundations, whose builder and maker is God," a kingdom which cannot be moved. Yes, men who call themselves learned and worldly wise, and good men too, alas! who fancy that they are preaching God's gospel, go about and tell men, 'The men of Babel were right after all. What have nations to do with God and religion? Nations are merely earthly, carnal things, that were only invented by sinful men themselves, to preserve their bodies and goods, and make trading easy. Religion has only to do with a man's private opinions, his single soul; the government has nothing to do with the Church: a Christian has nothing to do with politics.' And so these men most unwittingly open a door to all sorts of covetousness and meanness in the nation, and all sorts of trickery and cowardice in the government. Tell a man that his business has nothing to do with God, and you cannot wonder if he acts without thinking of God. If you tell a nation that it is selfishness which makes it prosperous, of course you must expect it to be selfish. If you tell us Englishmen that the duties of a citizen are not duties to God, but only duties to the constable and the tax-gatherer, what wonder if men believe you and become undutiful to God in their citizenship? No, my friends, once for all, as sure as God made Abraham a great nation, so if we English are a great nation, God has made us so—as sure as God gave Abraham the land of Canaan for his possession, so did *He* give us this land of England, when He brought our Saxon forefathers out of the wild barren north, and drove out before them nations greater and mightier than they, and gave them great and goodly cities which they builded not, and wells digged which they digged not, farms and gardens which they planted not, that we too might fear the Lord our God, and serve Him, and swear by His name;—as sure as He commanded Abraham to respect the property of his neighbours, so has He commanded us;—as sure as God taught Abraham that the nation which was to grow from him owed a duty to God, and could be only strong by faith in God, so it is with us: we, English people, owe a duty to God, and are to deal among ourselves, and with foreign countries, by faith in God, and in the fear of God, "seeking first the kingdom of God and His righteousness," sure that then all other things—victory, health, commerce, art, and science—will be added to us, as the first Lesson says. For this is your wisdom and understanding in the sight of the nations, which shall say, Surely this great nation is a wise and understanding people! For what nation is grown so great, that hath statutes and judgments so righteous as these laws, this gospel, which God sets before us day by day?—us, Englishmen!

And I say that these are proper thoughts for this place. This is not a mere preaching-house, where you may learn every man to save his own soul; this is a far nobler place; this building belongs to the National Church of England, and we worship here, not merely as men, but as men of England, citizens of a Christian country, come here to learn not merely how to save ourselves, but how to help towards the saving of our families, our parish, and our nation; and therefore we must know what a country and a nation mean, and what is the meaning of that glorious and divine word, "a citizen;" that by learning what it is to be a citizen of England, we may go on to learn fully what it is to be a citizen of the kingdom of God.

For this is part of the whole counsel of God, which He reveals in His Holy Bible; and this also we must not, and dare not, shun declaring in these days.

SERMON XIII.
ABRAHAM'S OBEDIENCE.

Hebrews, xi. 17–19.

"By faith Abraham, when he was tried, offered up Isaac; and he that had received the promises offered up his only-begotten son, of whom it was said, That in Isaac shall thy seed be called: accounting that God was able to raise him up, even from the dead; from whence also he received him in a figure."

In this chapter we come to the crowning point of Abraham's history, the highest step and perfection of his faith; beyond which it seems as if man's trust in God could no further go.

You know, most of you, doubtless, that Isaac, Abraham's son, was come to him out of the common course of nature—when he and his wife, Sarah, were of an age which seemed to make all chance of a family utterly hopeless. You remember how God promised Abraham that this boy should be born to him at a certain time, when He appeared to him on the plains of Mamre, in that most solemn and deep-meaning vision of which I spoke to you last Sunday. You remember, too, no doubt, most of you, how God had promised Abraham again and again, that in his seed, his children, all the nations of the earth should be blessed; so that all Abraham's hopes were wrapped up in this boy Isaac; he was his only son, whom he loved; he was the child of his old age, his glory and his joy; he was the child of God's promises. Every time Abraham looked at him he felt that Isaac was a wonderful child: that God had a great work for him to do; that from that single boy a great nation was to spring, as many in multitude as the stars in the sky, or the sand on the seashore, for the great Almighty God had said it. And he knew, too, that from that boy, who was growing up by him in his tent, all the nations in the earth should be blessed: so that Isaac, his son, was to Abraham a daily sacrament, as I may say, a sign and a pledge that God was with him, and would be true to him; that as surely as God had wonderfully and beyond all hope given him that son, so wonderfully and beyond all hope He would fulfil all His other promises. Conceive, then, if you can, what Abraham's astonishment, and doubt, and terror, and misery, must have been at such a message as this from the very God who had given Isaac to him: "And it came to pass after these things that God did tempt Abraham, and said unto him, Abraham: and he said, Behold, here I am. And he said, Take now thy son, thine only son Isaac, whom thou lovest, and get thee into the land of Moriah; and offer him there for a burnt-offering upon one of the mountains which I will tell thee of."

What a storm of doubt it must have raised in Abraham's mind! How unable he must have been to say whether that message came from a good or bad spirit, or commanded him to do a good action or a bad one; that the same God who had said, "Whoso sheddeth man's blood, by man shall his blood be shed;" who had forbidden murder as the very highest of crimes, should command him to shed the blood of his own son; that the same God who had promised him that in Isaac all the nations of the earth should be blessed, should command him to put to death that very son upon whom all his hopes depended! Fearful, indeed, must have been the struggle in Abraham's mind, but the good and the right thought conquered at last. His feeling was, no doubt, 'This God who has blessed me so long, who has guided me so long, whom I have obeyed so long, shall I not trust Him a little further yet? how can I believe that He will do wrong? how can I believe that He will lead me wrong? If it is really wrong that I should kill my son, He will not let me do it: if it really is His will that I should kill my son, *I will do it*. Whatever He says must be right; it is agony and misery to me, but what of that? Do I not owe Him a thousand daily and hourly blessings? Has He not led me hither, preserved me, guided me, taught me the knowledge of Himself,—chosen me to be the father of a great nation? Do I not owe Him everything? and shall I not bear this sharp sorrow for His sake? I know, too, that if Isaac dies, all my hope, all my joy, will die with him; that I shall have nothing left to look for, nothing left to work for in this world. Nothing! shall I not have God left to me? When Isaac is dead will the Lord die? will the Lord change? will He grow weak?—Never! Years ago did He declare to me that He was the Almighty God; I will believe that He will be always Almighty; I will believe that though I kill my son, my son will be still in God's hands, and I shall be still in God's hands, and that God is able to raise him again, even from the dead. God can give him back to me, and if He will *not* give him back to me, He can fulfil His promises in a thousand other ways. Ay, and He will fulfil His promises, for in Him is neither deceit, nor fickleness, nor weakness, nor unrighteousness of any kind; and, come what will, I will believe His promise and I will obey His will.'

Some such thoughts as these, I suppose, passed through Abraham's mind. He could not have had a man's heart in him indeed, if not only those thoughts, but ten thousand more, sadder, and stranger, and more pitiful than my weak brain can imagine, did not sweep like a storm through his soul at that last and terrible temptation, but the Bible tells us nothing of them: why should the Bible tell us anything of them? the Bible sets forth Abraham as the faithful man, and therefore it simply tells us of his faith, without telling us of his doubts and struggles before he settled down into faith. It tells us, as it were, not how often the wind shifted and twisted about during the tempest, but in what quarter the wind settled when the tempest was over, and it began to blow steadily, and fixedly, and gently, and all was bright, and mild, and still in Abraham's bosom again, just as a man's mind will be bright, and gentle, and calm, even at the moment he is going to certain death or fearful misery, if he does but know that his suffering is his duty, and that his trial is his heavenly Father's will: and so all we read in the Old-Testament account is simply, "And Abraham rose up early in the morning, and saddled his ass, and took two of his young men with him, and Isaac his son, and clave the wood for the burnt-offering, and rose up, and went unto the place of which God had told him. Then on the third day Abraham lifted up his eyes, and saw the place afar off. And Abraham said unto his young men, Abide ye here with the ass; and I and the lad will go yonder and worship, and come again to you. And Abraham took the wood of the burnt-offering, and laid it upon Isaac his son: and he took the fire in his hand, and a knife; and they went both of them together. And Isaac spake unto Abraham his father, and said, My father, and he said, Here am I, my son. And he said, Behold the fire and the wood, but where is the lamb for a burnt-offering? and Abraham said, My son, God will provide Himself a lamb for a burnt-offering. So they went both of them together. And they came to the place which God had told him of; and Abraham built an altar there, and laid the wood in order, and bound Isaac his son, and laid him on the altar upon the wood. And Abraham stretched forth his hand, and took the knife to slay his son."

Really if one is to consider the whole circumstances of Abraham's trials, they seem to have been infinite, more than mortal man could bear; more than he could have borne, no doubt, if the same God who tried had not rewarded his strength of mind by strengthening him still more, and rewarded his faith by increasing his faith; when we consider the struggle he must have had to keep the dreadful secret from the young man's mother, the tremendous effort of controlling himself, the long and frightful journey, the necessity, and yet the difficulty he seems to have felt of keeping the truth from his son, and yet of telling him the truth, which he did in those wonderful words, "God shall provide Himself a lamb for a burnt-offering" (on which I shall have occasion to speak presently); and, last and worst of all, the perfect obedience and submission of his son; for Isaac was not a child then, he was a young man of nearly thirty years of age; strong and able enough, no doubt, to have resisted his aged father, if he had chosen. But the very excellence of Isaac seems to have been, that he did not resist, that he shewed the same perfect trust and obedience to Abraham that Abraham did towards God; for he was led "as a lamb to the slaughter, and as a sheep before her shearers is dumb, so he opened not his mouth," for we read, "Abraham bound Isaac his son and laid him on the wood." Surely that was the bitterest pang of all, to see the excellence of his son shine forth just when it was too late for him to enjoy him—to find out what a perfect child he had, in simple trust and utter obedience, just at the very moment when he was going to lose him: "And Abraham stretched forth his hand and took the knife to slay his son."

At that point Abraham's trial finished. He had shewn the completeness of his faith by the completeness of his works, that is, by the completeness of his obedience. He had utterly given up all for God. He had submitted his will completely to God's will. He had said in heart, as our Blessed Lord said, "Father, if it be possible, let this woe pass from me, nevertheless, not as I will, but as Thou wilt;" and thus I say, he was justified by his works, by his actions; that is, by this faithful action he proved the faithfulness of his heart, as the Angel said to him, "Now I know that thou fearest God, seeing thou hast not withheld thy son, thine only son from me:" for as St. James says, "Was not Abraham our father justified by works when he had offered Isaac his son upon the altar? Seest thou," says he, "how his faith wrought with his works;" how his works were the tool or instrument which his faith used; and by his works his faith was brought to perfection, as a tree is brought to perfection when it bears fruit. "And so," St. James continues, "the scripture was fulfilled, which says, Abraham believed God, and it was imputed to him for righteousness; and he was called the friend of God. Ye see then," he says, "how that by works a man is justified," or shewn to be righteous and faithful, "and not by faith only;" that is, not by the mere feeling of faith, for, as he says, "as the body without the spirit is dead, so faith without works is dead also." For what is the sign of a being dead? It is its not being able to do anything, not being able to work; because there is no living and moving spirit in it. And what is the sign of a man's faith being dead? his faith not being able to *work*, because there is no living spirit in it, but it is a mere dead, empty shell and form of words,—a mere notion and thought about believing in a man's head, but not a living trust and loyalty to God in his heart. Therefore, says St. James, "shew me thy faith without thy works," if thou canst, "and I will shew thee my faith by my works," as Abraham did by offering up Isaac his son.

Oh! my friends, when people are talking about faith and works, and trying to reconcile St. Paul and St. James, as they call it, because St. Paul says Abraham was justified by faith, and St. James says Abraham was justified by works, if they would but pray for the simple, childlike heart, and the head of common sense, and look at their own children, who, every time they go on a message for them, settle, without knowing it, this mighty difference of man's making between faith and works. You tell a little child daily to do many things the meaning and use of which it cannot understand; and the child has faith in what you tell it; and, therefore, it does what you tell it, and so it shews its faith in you by obedience in working for you.

But to go on with the verses: "And the angel of the Lord called unto Abraham out of heaven the second time, and said, By myself have I sworn, saith the Lord, for because thou hast done this thing, and hast not withheld thy son, thine only son: that in blessing I will bless thee, and in multiplying I will multiply thy seed as the stars of the heaven, and as the sand which is upon the sea-shore; and thy seed shall possess the gate of his enemies; and in thy seed shall all the nations of the earth be blessed; because thou hast obeyed my voice."

Now, here remark two things; first, that it was Abraham's obedience in giving up all to God, which called forth from God this confirmation of God's promises to him; and next, that God here promised him nothing new; God did not say to him, 'Because thou hast obeyed me in this great matter, I will give thee some great reward over and above what I promised thee.' No; God merely promises him over again, but more solemnly than ever, what He had promised him many years before.

And so it will be with us, my friends, we must not expect to *buy* God's favour by obeying Him,—we must not expect that the more we do for God, the more God will be bound to do for us, as the Papists do. No; God has done for us all that He will do. He has promised us all that He will promise. He has provided us, as He provided Abraham, a lamb for the burnt-offering, the Lamb without blemish and without spot, which taketh away the sins of the world. We are His redeemed people—we *have* a share in His promises—He bids us believe *that*, and shew that we believe it by living as redeemed men, not our own, but bought with a price, and created anew in Christ Jesus to do good works; not that we may buy forgiveness by them, but that we may shew by them that we believe that God *has* forgiven us already, and that when we have done all that is commanded us, we are still unprofitable servants; for though we should give up at God's bidding our children, our wives, and our own limbs and lives, and shew as utter faith in God, and complete obedience to God, as Abraham did, we should only have done just what it was already our duty to do.

SERMON XIV.
OUR FATHER IN HEAVEN.

1 JOHN, ii. 13.

"I write unto you, little children, because ye have known the Father."

I PREACHED some time ago a sermon on the whole of these most deep and blessed verses of St. John.

I now wish to speak to those who are of age to be confirmed three separate sermons on three separate parts of these verses. First to those whom St. John calls little children; next, to those whom He calls grown men. To the first I will speak to-day; to the latter, by God's help, next Sunday. And may the Blessed One bring home my weak words to all your hearts!

Now for the meaning of "little children." There are those who will tell you that those words mean merely "weak believers," "babes in grace," and so on. They mean that, no doubt; but they mean much more. They mean, first of all, be sure, what they say. St. John would not have said "little children," if he had not meant little children. Surely God's apostle did not throw about his words at random, so as to leave them open to mistakes, and want some one to step in and tell us that they do not mean their plain, common-sense meaning, but something else. Holy Scripture is too wisely written, and too awful a matter, to be trifled with in that way, and cut and squared to suit our own fancies, and explained away, till its blessed promises are made to mean anything or nothing.

No! By little children, St. John means here children in age,—of course *Christian* children and young people, for he was writing only to Christians. He speaks to those who have been christened, and brought up, more or less, as christened children should be. But, no doubt, when he says little children, he means also all Christian people, whether they be young or old, whose souls are still young, and weak, and unlearned. All, however old they may be, who have not been confirmed—I do not merely mean confirmed by the bishop, but confirmed by God's grace,—all those who have not yet come to a full knowledge of their own sins,—all who have not yet been converted, and turned to God with their whole hearts and wills, who have not yet made their full choice between God and sin,—all who have not yet fought for themselves the battle which no man or angel can fight for them—I mean the battle between their selfishness and their duty—the battle between their love of pleasure and their fear of sin—the battle, in short, between the devil and his temptations to darkness and shame, and God and His promises of light, and strength, and glory,—all who have not been converted to God, to them St. John speaks as little children—people who are not yet strong enough to stand alone, and do their duty on God's side against sin, the world, and the devil. And all of you here who have not yet made up your minds, who have not yet been confirmed in soul,—whether you were confirmed by the bishop or not,—to you I speak this day.

Now, first of all, consider this,—that though St. John calls you "little children," because you are still weak, and your souls have not grown to manhood, yet he does not speak to you as if you were heathens and knew nothing about God; he says, "I have written unto you, little children, because ye have known the Father." Consider that; that was his reason for all that he had written to them before; that they had known the Father, the God who made heaven and earth—the Father of our Lord Jesus Christ—the Father of little children—my Father and your Father, my friends, little as we may behave like what we are, sons of the Almighty God. That was St. John's reason for speaking to little children, because they had already known the Father. So he does not speak to them as if they were heathens; and I dare not speak to you, young people, as if you were heathens, however foolish and sinful some of you may be; I dare not do it, whatever many preachers may do nowadays; not because I should be unfair and hard upon you merely, but because I should lie, and deny the great grace and mercy which God has shewn you, and count the blood of the covenant, with which you were sprinkled at baptism, an unholy thing; and do despite to the spirit of grace which has been struggling in your hearts, trying to lead you out of sin into good, out of light into darkness, ever since you were born. Therefore, as St. John said, I say, I preach this day to you, young people, because you have known your Father in heaven!

But some of you may say to me, 'You put a great honour on us; but we do not see that we have any right to it. You tell us that we have a very noble and awful knowledge—that we know the Father. We are afraid that we do not know Him; we do not even rightly understand of whom or what you preach.'

Well, my young friends, these are very awful words of St. John; such blessed and wonderful words, that if we did not find them in the Bible, it would be madness and insolence to God of us to say such a thing, not merely of little children, but even of the greatest, and wisest, and holiest man who ever lived; but there they are in the Bible—the blessed Lord Himself has told us all, "When ye pray, say, Our Father in heaven;"—and I dare not keep them back because they sound strange. They may *sound* strange, but they *are not* strange. Any one who has ever watched a young child's heart, and seen how naturally and at once the little innocent takes in the thought of his Father which is in heaven, knows that it is not a strange thought—that it comes to a little child almost by instinct—that his Father in heaven seems often to be just the thought which fills his heart most completely, has most power over him,—the thought which has been lying ready in his heart all the time, only waiting for some one to awaken it, and put it into words for him; that he will do right when you put him in mind of his Father above the skies sooner than he will for a hundred punishments. For truly says the poet,—

> "Heaven lies about us in our infancy,
> Not in complete forgetfulness,
> Nor yet in utter nakedness,
> But trailing clouds of glory do we come,
> From God who is our home!"

And yet more truly said the Blessed One Himself, "That children's angels always behold the face of our Father which is in heaven;" and that "of such is the kingdom of heaven." Yet you say, some of you, perhaps, 'Whatever knowledge of our Father in heaven we had, or ought to have had, when we were young, we have lost it now. We have forgotten what we learnt at school. We have been what you would call sinful; at all events, we have been thinking all our time about a great many things beside religion, and they have quite put out of our head the thought that God is our Father. So how have we known our Father in heaven?'

Well, then, to answer that,—consider the case of your earthly fathers, the men who begot you and brought you up. Now there might be one of you who had never seen his father since he was born, but all he knows of him is, that his name is so and so, and that he is such and such a sort of man, as the case might be; and that he lives in such and such a place, far away, and that now and then he hears talk of his father, or receives letters or presents from him. Suppose I asked that young man, Do you know your father? would he not answer—would he not have a right to answer, 'Yes, I know him. I never saw him, or was acquainted with him, but I know him well enough; I know who he is, and where to find him, and what sort of a man he is.' That young man might not know his father's face, or love him, or care for him at all. He might have been disobedient to his father; he might have forgotten for years that he had a father at all, and might have lived on his own way, just as if he had no father. But when he was put in mind of it all, would he not say at once, 'Yes, I know my father well enough; his name is so and so, and he lives at such and such a place. I know my father.'

Well, my young friends, and if this would be true of your fathers on earth, it is just as true of your Father in heaven. You have never seen Him—you may have forgotten Him—you may have disobeyed Him—you may have lived on your own way, as if you had no Father in heaven; still you know that you have a Father in heaven. You pray, surely, sometimes. What do you say? "Our Father which art in heaven." So you have a Father in heaven, else what right have you to use those words,—what right have you to say to God, "Our Father in heaven," if you believe that you have no Father there? That would be only blasphemy and mockery. I can well understand that you have often said those words without thinking of them—without thinking what a blessed, glorious, soul-saving meaning there was in them; but I will not believe that you never once in your whole lives said, "Our Father which art in heaven," without believing them to be true words. What I want is, for you *always* to believe them to be true. Oh young men and young women, boys and girls—believe those words, believe that when you say, "Our Father which art in heaven," you speak God's truth about yourselves; that the evil devil rages when he hears you speak those words, because they are the words which prove that you do not belong to him and to hell, but to God and the kingdom of heaven. Oh, believe those words—behave as if you believed those words, and you shall see what will come of them, through all eternity for ever.

Well, but you will ask, What has all this to do with confirmation? It has all to do with confirmation. Because you are God's children, and know that you are God's children, you are to go and confirm before the bishop your right to be called God's children. You are to go and claim your share in God's kingdom. If you were heir to an estate, you would go and claim your estate from those who held it. You are heirs to an estate—you are heirs to the kingdom of heaven; go to confirmation, and claim that kingdom, say, 'I am a citizen of God's kingdom. Before the bishop and the congregation, here I proclaim the honour which God has put upon me.' If you have a father, you will surely not be ashamed to own him! How much more when the Almighty God of heaven is your Father! You will not be ashamed to own Him? Then go to confirmation; for by doing so you own God for your Father. If you have an earthly father, you will not be ashamed to say, 'I know I ought to honour him and obey him;' how much more when your father is the Almighty God of heaven, who sent His own Son into the world to die for you, who is daily heaping you with blessings body and soul! You will not be ashamed to confess that you ought to honour and obey Him? Then go to confirmation, and say, 'I here take upon myself the vow and promise made for me at my baptism. I am God's child, and therefore I will honour, love, and obey Him. It is my duty; and it shall be my delight henceforward to work for God, to do all the good I can to my life's end, because my Father in heaven loves the good, and has commanded me, poor, weak countryman though I be, to work for Him in well-doing.' So I say, If God is your Father, go and own Him at confirmation. If God is your Father, go and promise to love and obey Him at confirmation; and see if He does not, like a strong and loving Father as He is, confirm you in return,—see if He does not give you strength of heart, and peace of mind, and clear, quiet, pure thoughts, such as a man or woman ought to have who considers that the great God, who made the sky and stars above their heads, is their Father. But, perhaps, there are some of you, young people, who do not wish to be confirmed. And why? Now, look honestly into your own hearts and see the reason. Is it not, after all, because you don't like the *trouble*? Because you are afraid that being confirmed will force you to think seriously and be religious; and you had rather not take all that trouble yet? Is it not because you do not like to look your ownselves in the face, and see how foolishly you have been living, and how many bad habits you will have to give up, and what a thorough conversion and change you must make, if you are to be confirmed in earnest? Is not this why you do not wish to be confirmed? And what does that all come to? That though you know you are God's children, you do not like to tell people publicly that you are God's children, lest they should expect you to behave like God's children—that is it. Now, young men and young women, think seriously once for all—if you have any common *sense*—I do not say grace, left in you—think! Are you not playing a fearful game? You would not dare to deny your fathers on earth—to refuse to obey them, because you know well enough that they would punish you—that if you were too old for punishment, your neighbours, at least, would despise you for mean, ungrateful, and rebellious children! But because you cannot *see* God your Father, because you have not some sign or wonder hanging in the sky to frighten you into good behaviour, therefore you are not afraid to turn your backs on him. My friends, it is ill mocking the living God. Mark my words! If a man will not turn He will whet His sword, and make us feel it. You who can be confirmed, and know in your hearts that you ought to be confirmed, and ought to be *really* converted and confirmed in soul, and make no mockery of it,—mark my words! If you will not be converted and confirmed of your own good will, God, if He has any love left for you, will convert and confirm you against your will. He will let you go your own ways till you find out your own folly. He will bring you low with affliction perhaps, with sickness, with ill-luck, with shame. Some way or other, He will chastise you, again and again, till you are forced to come back to Him, and take His service on you. If He loves you, He will drive you home to your Father's house. You may laugh at my words now, see if you laugh at them when your hairs are grey. Oh, young people, if you wish in after-life to save yourselves shame and sorrow, and perhaps, in the world to come eternal death, come to confirmation, acknowledge God for your Father, promise to come and serve Him faithfully, make those blessed words of the Lord's Prayer, "Our Father in heaven," your glory and your honour, your guide and guard through life, your title-deeds to heaven. You who know that the Great God is your Father, will you be ashamed to own yourselves His sons?

SERMON XV.
THE TRANSFIGURATION.

MARK, ix. 2.

"Jesus taketh Peter, and James, and John, and leadeth them up into a high mountain apart, and was transfigured before them."

THE second lesson for this morning service brings us to one of the most wonderful passages in our blessed Saviour's whole stay on earth, namely, His transfiguration. The story, as told by the different Evangelists, is this,—That our Lord took Peter, and John, and James his brother, and led them up into a high mountain apart, which mountain may be seen to this very day. It is a high peaked hill, standing apart from all the hills around it, with a small smooth space of ground upon the top, very fit, from its height and its loneliness, for a transaction like the transfiguration, which our Lord wished no one but these three to behold. There the apostles fell asleep; while our blessed Lord, who had deeper thoughts in His heart than they had, knelt down and prayed to *His* Father and *our* Father, which is in heaven. And as He prayed, the form of His countenance was changed, and His raiment became shining, white as the light; and there appeared Moses and Elijah talking with Him. They talked of matters which the angels desire to look into, of the greatest matters that ever happened in this earth since it was made; of the redemption of the world, and of the death which Christ was to undergo at Jerusalem. And as they were talking, the apostles awoke, and found into what glorious company they had fallen while they slept. What they felt no mortal man can tell—that moment was worth to them all the years they had lived before. When they had gone up with Jesus into the mount, He was but the poor carpenter's son, wonderful enough to *them*, no doubt, with His wise, searching words, and His gentle, loving looks, that drew to Him all men who had hearts left in them, and wonderful enough, too, from all the mighty miracles which they had seen Him do, but still He was merely a man like themselves, poor, and young, and homeless, who felt the heat, and the cold, and the rough roads, as much as they did. They could feel that He spake as never man spake—they could see that God's spirit and power was on Him as it had never been on any man in their time. God had even enlightened their reason by His Spirit, to know that He was the Christ, the Son of the living God. But still it does seem they did not fully understand who and what He was; they could not understand how the Son of God should come in the form of a despised and humble man; they did not understand that His glory was to be a spiritual glory. They expected His kingdom to be a kingdom of this world—they expected His glory to consist in palaces, and armies, and riches, and jewels, and all the magnificence with which Solomon and the old Jewish kings were adorned; they thought that He was to conquer back again from the Roman emperor all the inestimable treasures of which the Romans had robbed the Jews, and that He was to make the Jewish nation, like the Roman, the conquerors and masters of all the nations of the earth. So that it was a puzzling thing to their minds why He should be King of the Jews at the very time that He was but a poor tradesman's son, living on charity. It was to shew them that His kingdom was the kingdom of heaven that He was transfigured before them.

They saw His glory—the glory as of the only-begotten of the Father, full of grace and truth. The form of His countenance was changed; all the majesty, and courage, and wisdom, and love, and resignation, and pity, that lay in His noble heart, shone out through His face, while He spoke of His death which He should accomplish at Jerusalem—the Holy Ghost that was upon Him, the spirit of wisdom, and love, and beauty—the spirit which produces every thing that is lovely in heaven and earth: in soul and body, blazed out through His eyes, and all His glorious countenance, and made Him look like what He was—a God. My friends, what a sight! Would it not be worth while to journey thousands of miles—to go through all difficulties, dangers, that man ever heard of, for one sight of that glorious face, that we might fall down upon our knees before it, and, if it were but for a moment, give way to the delight of finding something that we could utterly love and utterly adore? I say, the delight of finding something to worship; for if there is a noble, if there is a holy, if there is a spiritual feeling in man, it is the feeling which bows him down before those who are greater, and wiser, and holier than himself. I say, that feeling of respect for what is noble is a heavenly feeling. The man who has lost it—the man who feels no respect for those who are above him in age, above him in knowledge, above him in wisdom, above him in goodness,—*that* man shall in no wise enter into the kingdom of heaven. It is only the man who is like a little child, and feels the delight of having some one to look up to, who will ever feel delight in looking up to Jesus Christ, who is the Lord of lords and King of kings. It was the want of respect, it was the dislike of feeling any one superior to himself, which made the devil rebel against God, and fall from heaven. It will be the feeling of complete respect—the feeling of kneeling at the feet of one who is immeasurably superior to ourselves in every thing, that will make up the greatest happiness of heaven. This is a hard saying, and no man can understand it, save he to whom it is given by the Spirit of God.

That the apostles *had* this feeling of immeasurable respect for Christ there is no doubt, else they would never have been apostles. But they felt more than this. There were other wonders in that glorious vision besides the countenance of our Lord. His raiment, too, was changed, and became all brilliant, white as the light itself. Was not *that* a lesson to them? Was it not as if our Lord had said to them, 'I am a king, and have put on glorious apparel, but whence does the glory of my raiment come? *I* have no need of fine linen, and purple, and embroidery, the work of men's hands; *I* have no need to send my subjects to mines and caves to dig gold and jewels to adorn my crown: the earth is mine and the fulness thereof. All this glorious earth, with its trees and its flowers, its sunbeams and its storms, is *mine*. *I* made it—*I* can do what I will with it. All the mysterious laws by which the light and the heat flow out for ever from God's throne, to lighten the sun, and the moon, and the stars of heaven—they are mine. *I* am the light of the world—the light of men's bodies as well of their souls; and here is my proof of it. Look at Me. I am He that "decketh Himself with light as it were with a garment, who layeth the beams of His chambers in the waters, and walketh upon the wings of the wind." This was the message which Christ's glory brought the apostles—a message which they could never forget. The spiritual glory of His countenance had shewn them that He was a spiritual king—that His strength lay in the spirit of power, and wisdom, and beauty, and love, which God had given Him without measure; and it shewed them, too, that there was such a thing as a spiritual body, such a body as each of us some day shall have if we be found in Christ at the resurrection of the just—a body which shall not hide a man's spirit, when it becomes subject to the wear and tear of life, and disease, and decay; but a spiritual body—a body which shall be filled with our spirits, which shall be perfectly obedient to our spirits—a body through which the glory of our spirits shall shine out, as the glory of Christ's spirit shone out through His body at the transfiguration. "Brethren, we know not yet what we shall be, but this we do know, that when He shall appear, we shall be *like Him*, for we shall see Him as He is." (1 John, iii. 3.)

Thus our Lord taught them by His appearance that there is such a thing as a spiritual body, while, by the glory of His raiment, in addition to His other miracles, He taught them that He had power over the laws of nature, and could, in His own good time, "change the bodies of their humiliation, that they might be made like unto His glorious body, according to the mighty working by which He is able to subdue all things to Himself."

But there was yet another lesson which the apostles learnt from the transfiguration of our Lord. They beheld Moses and Elijah talking with Him:—Moses the great lawgiver of their nation, Elijah the chief of all the Jewish prophets. We must consider this a little to find out the whole depth of its meaning. You remember how Christ had spoken of Himself as having come, not to destroy the Law and the Prophets, but to fulfil them. You remember, too, how He had always said that He was the person of whom the Law and the Prophets had spoken.

Here was an actual sign and witness that His words were true—here was Moses, the giver of the Law, and Elijah, the chief of the Prophets, talking with Him, bearing witness to Him in their own persons, and shewing, too, that it was His death and His perfect sacrifice that they had been shadowing forth in the sacrifices of the law and in the dark speeches of prophecy. For they talked with Him of His death, which He was to accomplish at Jerusalem. What more perfect testimony could the apostles have had to shew them that Jesus of Nazareth, their Master, was He of whom the Law and the Prophets spoke—that He was indeed the Christ for whom Moses and Elijah, and all the saints of old, had looked; and that He was come not to destroy the Law and the Prophets, but to fulfil them? We can hardly understand the awe and the delight with which the disciples must have beheld those blessed Three—Moses, and Elias, and Jesus Christ, their Lord, talking together before their very eyes. For of all men in the world, Moses and Elias were to them the greatest. All true-hearted Israelites, who knew the history of their nation, and understood the promises of God, must have felt that Moses and Elias were the two greatest heroes and saviours of their nation, whom God had ever yet raised up. And the joy and the honour of thus seeing them face to face, the very men whom they had loved and reverenced in their thoughts, whom they had heard and read of from their childhood, as the greatest ornaments and glories of their nation—the joy and the honour, I say, of that unexpected sight, added to the wonderful majesty which was suddenly revealed to their transfigured Lord, seemed to have been too much for them—they knew not what to say. Such company seemed to them for the moment heaven enough; and St. Peter first finding words exclaimed, "Lord, it is good for us to be here. If thou wilt let us build three tabernacles, one for Thee, and one for Moses, and one for Elias." Not, I fancy, that they intended to worship Moses and Elias, but that they felt that Moses and Elias, as well as Christ, had each a divine message, which must be listened to; and therefore, they wished that each of them might have his own tabernacle, and dwell among men, and each teach his own particular doctrine and wisdom in his own school. It may seem strange that they should put Moses and Elias so on an equality with Christ, but the truth was, that as yet they understood Moses and Elias better than they did Christ. They had heard and read of Moses and Elijah all their lives—they were acquainted with all their actions and words—they knew thoroughly what great and noble men the Spirit of God had made them, but they did *not* understand Christ in like manner. They did not yet *feel* that God had given Him the Spirit without measure—they did not understand that He was not only to be a lawgiver and a prophet, but a sacrifice for sin, the conqueror of death and hell, who was to lead captivity captive, and receive inestimable gifts for men. Much less did they think that Moses and Elijah were but His servants—that all *their* spirit and *their* power had been given by Him. But this also they were taught a moment afterwards;

for a bright cloud overshadowed them, hiding from them the glory of God the Father, whom no man hath seen or can see, who dwells in the light which no man can approach unto; and out of that cloud, a voice saying, "This is my beloved Son; hear ye Him;" and then, hiding their faces in fear and wonder, they fell to the ground; and when they looked up, the vision and the voice had alike passed away, and they saw no man but Christ alone. Was not that enough for them? Must not the meaning of the vision have been plain to them? They surely understood from it that Moses and Elijah were, as they had ever believed them to be, great and good, true messengers of the living God; but that their message and their work was done—that Christ, whom they had looked for, was come—that all the types of the law were realised, and all the prophecies fulfilled, and that henceforward Christ, and Christ alone, was to be their Prophet and their Lawgiver. Was not this plainly the meaning of the Divine voice? For when they wished to build three tabernacles, and to honour Moses and Elijah, the Law and the Prophets, as separate from Christ—that moment the heavenly voice warned them: '*This*— *this* is my beloved Son—hear ye *Him*, and Him only, henceforward.' And Moses and Elijah, their work being done, forthwith vanished away, leaving Christ alone to fulfil the Law and the prophets, and all other wisdom and righteousness that ever was or shall be. This is another lesson which Christ's transfiguration was meant to teach and us, that Christ alone is to be henceforward our guide; that no philosophies or doctrines of any sort which are not founded on a true faith in Jesus Christ, and His life and death, are worth listening to; that God has manifested forth His beloved Son, and that Him, and Him only, we are to hear. I do not mean to say that Christ came into the world to put down human learning. I do not mean that we are to despise human learning, as so many are apt to do nowadays; for Christ came into the world not to destroy human learning, but to fulfil it—to sanctify it— to make human learning true, and strong, and useful, by giving it a sure foundation to stand upon, which is the belief and knowledge of His blessed self. Just as Christ came not to destroy the Law and the Prophets, but to fulfil them—to give them a spirit and a depth in men's eyes which they never had before—just so, He came to fulfil all true philosophies, all the deep thoughts which men had ever thought about this wonderful world and their own souls, by giving *them* a spirit and a depth which *they* never had before. Therefore let no man tempt you to despise learning, for it is holy to the Lord.

There is one more lesson which we may learn from our Lord's transfiguration; when St. Peter said, "*Lord!* it is good for us to be here," he spoke a truth. It *was* good for him to be there; nevertheless, Christ did not listen to his prayer. He and his two companions were not allowed to *stay* in that glorious company. And why? Because they had a work to do. They had glad tidings of great joy to proclaim to every creature, and it was, after all, but a selfish prayer, to wish to be allowed to stay in ease and glory on the mount while the whole world was struggling in sin and wickedness below them: for there is no meaning in a man's calling himself a Christian, or saying that he loves God, unless he is ready to hate what God hates, and to fight against that which Christ fought against, that is, sin. No one has any right to call himself a servant of God, who is not trying to do away with some of the evil in the world around him. And, therefore, Christ was merciful, when, instead of listening to St. Peter's prayer, He led the apostles down again from the mount, and sent them forth, as He did afterwards, to preach the Gospel of the kingdom to all nations. For Christ put a higher honour on St. Peter by that than if He had let him stay on the mount all his life, to behold His glory, and worship and adore. And He made St. Peter more like Himself by doing so. For what was Christ's life? Not one of deep speculations, quiet thoughts, and bright visions, such as St. Peter wished to lead; but a life of fighting against evil; earnest, awful prayers and struggles within, continual labour of body and mind without, insult and danger, and confusion, and violent exertion, and bitter sorrow. This was Christ's life—this is the life of almost every good man I ever heard of;—this was St. Peter, and St. James, and St. John's life afterwards. This was Christ's cup, which they were to drink of as well as He;—this was the baptism of fire with which they were to be baptised of as well as He;—this was to be their fight of faith;—this was the tribulation through which they, like all other great saints, were to enter into the kingdom of heaven; for it is certain that the harder a man fights against evil, the harder evil will fight against him in return: but it is certain, too, that the harder a man fights against evil, the more he is like his Saviour Christ, and the more glorious will be his reward in heaven. It is certain, too, that what was good for St. Peter is good for us. It is good for a man to have holy and quiet thoughts, and at moments to see into the very deepest meaning of God's word and God's earth, and to have, as it were, heaven opened before his eyes; and it is good for a man sometimes actually to *feel* his heart overpowered with the glorious majesty of God, and to *feel* it gushing out with love to his blessed Saviour: but it is not good for him to stop there, any more than it was for the apostles; they had to leave that glorious vision and come down from the mount, and do Christ's work; and *so have we*; for, believe me, one word of warning spoken to keep a little child out of sin,—one crust of bread given to a beggar-man, because he is your brother, for whom Christ died,—one angry word checked, when it is on your lips, for the sake of Him who was meek and lowly in heart; in short, any, the smallest endeavour of this kind to lessen the quantity of evil, which is in yourselves, and in those around you, is worth all the speculations, and raptures, and visions, and frames, and feelings in the world; for those are the good *fruits* of faith, whereby alone the tree shall be known whether it be good or evil.

SERMON XVI.
THE CRUCIFIXION.

Isaiah, liii. 7.

"He is brought as a lamb to the slaughter."

ON this day, my friends, was offered up upon the cross the Lamb of God,—slain in eternity and heaven before the foundation of the world, but slain in time and space upon this day. All the old sacrifices, the lambs which were daily offered up to God in the Jewish Temple, the lambs which Abel, and after him the patriarchs offered up, the Paschal Lamb slain at the Passover, our Eastertide, all these were but figures of Christ—tokens of the awful and yet loving law of God, that without shedding of blood there is no remission of sin. But the blood of dumb animals could not take away sin. All mankind had sinned, and it was, therefore, necessary that all mankind should suffer. Therefore He suffered, the new Adam, the Man of all men, in whom all mankind were, as it were, collected into one and put on a new footing with God; that henceforward to be a man might mean to be a holy being, a forgiven being, a being joined to God, wearing the likeness of the Son of God—the human soul and body in which He offered up all human souls and bodies on the cross. For man was originally made in Christ's likeness; He was the Word of God who walked in the garden of Eden, who spoke to Adam with a human voice; He was the Lord who appeared to the patriarchs in a man's figure, and ate and drank in Abraham's tent, and spoke to him with a human voice; He was the God of Israel, whom the Jewish elders saw with their bodily eyes upon Mount Sinai, and under His feet a pavement as of a sapphire stone. From Him all man's powers came—man's speech, man's understanding. All that is truly noble in man was a dim pattern of Him in whose likeness man was originally made. And when man had fallen and sinned, and Christ's image was fading more and more out of him, and the likeness of the brutes growing more and more in him year by year, then came Christ, the head and the original pattern of all men, to claim them for His own again, to do in their name what they could never do for themselves, to offer Himself up a sacrifice for the sins of the whole world: so that He is the real sacrifice, the real lamb; as St. John said when he pointed Him out to his disciples, "Behold the Lamb of God, which taketh away the sin of the world!"

Oh, think of that strong and patient Lamb, who on this day shewed Himself perfect in fortitude and nobleness, perfect in meekness and resignation. Think of Him who, in His utter love to us, endured the cross, despising the shame. And what a cross! Truly said the prophet, "His visage was marred more than any man, and His form more than the sons of men:" in hunger and thirst, in tears and sighs, bruised and bleeding, His forehead crowned with thorns, His sides torn with scourges, His hands and feet gored with nails, His limbs stretched from their sockets, naked upon the shameful cross, the Son of God hung, lingering slowly towards the last gasp, in the death of the felon and the slave! The most shameful sight that this earth ever saw, and yet the most glorious sight. The most shameful sight, at which the sun in heaven veiled his face, as if ashamed, and the skies grew black, as if to hide those bleeding limbs from the foul eyes of men; and yet the noblest sight, for in that death upon the cross shone out the utter fullness of all holiness, the utter fullness of all fortitude, the utter fullness of that self-sacrificing love, which had said, "The Son of Man came to seek and to save that which was lost;" the utter fullness of obedient patience, which could say, "Father, not My will but Thine be done;" the utter fullness of generous forgiveness, which could pray, "Father, forgive them, for they know not what they do;" the utter fullness of noble fortitude and endurance, which could say at the very moment when a fearful death stared Him in the face, "Thinkest thou that I cannot now pray to the Father, and He will send me at once more than twelve armies of angels? But how then would the Scriptures be fulfilled that thus it must be?"

Oh, my friends, look to Him, the author and perfecter of all faith, all trust, all loyal daring for the sake of duty and of God! Look at His patience. See how He endured the cross, despising the shame. See how He endured—how patience had her perfect work in Him—how in all things He was more than conqueror. What gentleness, what calmness, what silence, what infinite depths of Divine love within Him! A heart which neither shame, nor torture, nor insult, could stir from its Godlike resolution. When looking down from that cross He beheld none almost but enemies, heard no word but mockery; when those who passed by reviled Him, wagging their heads and saying, "He saved others, Himself He cannot save;" His only answer was a prayer for forgiveness for that besotted mob who were yelling beneath Him like hounds about their game. Consider Him, and then consider ourselves, ruffled and put out of temper by the slightest cross accident, the slightest harsh word, too often by the slightest pain—not to mention insults, for we pride ourselves in not bearing them. Try, my friends, if you can, even in the dimmest way, fancy yourselves for one instant in His place this day 1815 years. Fancy yourselves hanging on that cross—fancy that mocking mob below—fancy—but I dare not go on with the picture. Only think—think what would have been *your* temper there, and then you may get some slight notion of the boundless love and the boundless endurance of the Saviour whom *we* love so little, for whose sake most of us will not endure the trouble of giving up a single sin.

And then consider that it was all of His own free will; that at any moment, even while He was hanging upon the cross, He might have called to earth and sun, to heaven and to hell, "Stop! thus far, but no further," and they would have obeyed Him; and all that cross, and agony, and the fierce faces of those furious Jews, would have vanished away like a hideous dream when one awakes. For they lied in their mockery. Any moment He might have been free, triumphant, again in His eternal bliss, but He would not. He Himself kept Himself on that cross till His Father's will was fulfilled, and the sacrifice was finished, and we were saved. And then at last, when there was no more human nobleness, no more agony left for Him to fulfil, no gem in the crown of holiness which He had not won as His own, no drop in the cup of misery which He had not drained as His own; when at last He was made perfect through suffering, and His strength had been made perfect in weakness, then He bowed that bleeding, thorn-crowned head, and said, "It is finished. Father, into Thy hands I commend my spirit." And so He died.

How can our poor words, our poor deeds, thank Him? How mean and paltry our deepest gratitude, our highest loyalty, when compared with Him to whom it is due—that adorable victim, that perfect sin-offering, who this day offered up Himself upon the altar of the cross, in the fire of His own boundless zeal for the kingdom of God, His Father, and of His boundless love for us, His sinful brothers! "Oh, thou blessed Jesus! Saviour, agonising for us! God Almighty, who did make Thyself weak for the love of us! oh, write that love upon our hearts so deeply that neither pleasure nor sorrow, life nor death, may wipe it away! Thou hast sacrificed Thyself for us, oh, give us the hearts to sacrifice ourselves for Thee! Thou art the Vine, we are the branches. Let Thy priceless blood shed for us on this day flow like life-giving sap through all our hearts and minds, and fill us with Thy righteousness, that we may be sacrifices fit for Thee. Stir us up to offer to Thee, O Lord, our bodies, our souls, our spirits, in all we love and all we learn, in all we plan and all we do, to offer our labours, our pleasures, our sorrows, to Thee; to work for Thy kingdom through them, to live as those who are not their own, but bought with Thy blood, fed with Thy body; and enable us now, in Thy most holy Sacrament, to offer to Thee our repentance, our faith, our prayers, our praises, living, reasonable, and spiritual sacrifices,—Thine from our birth-hour, Thine now, and Thine for ever!"

SERMON XVII.
THE RESURRECTION.

LUKE, xxiv. 6.

"He is not here—He is risen."

WE are assembled here to-day, my friends, to celebrate the joyful memory of our blessed Saviour's Resurrection. All Friday night, Saturday, and Saturday night, His body lay in the grave; His soul was—where we cannot tell. St. Peter tells us that He went and preached to the spirits in prison—the sinners of the old world, who are kept in the place of departed souls—most likely in the depths of the earth, in the great fire-kingdom, which boils and flames miles below our feet, and breaks out here and there through the earth's solid crust in burning mountains and streams of fire. There some say—and the Bible seems to say—sinful souls are kept in chains until the judgment-day; and thither they say Christ went to preach—no doubt to save some of those sinful souls who had never heard of Him. However this may be, for those two nights and day there was no sign, no stir in the grave where Christ was laid. His body seemed dead—the stone lay still over the mouth of the tomb where Joseph and Nicodemus laid him; the seal which Pilate had put on it was unbroken; the soldiers watched and watched, but no one stirred; the priests and Pharisees were keeping their sham Passover, thinking, no doubt, that they were well rid of Christ and of His rebukes for ever.

But early on the Sunday morn—this day, as it might be—in the grey dawn of morning there came a change—a wondrous change. There was a great earthquake; the solid ground and rocks were stirred—the angel of the Lord came down from heaven, and rolled back the stone from the door, and sat upon it, waiting for the King of glory to arise from His slumber, and go forth the conqueror of Death.

His countenance was like lightning, and His raiment white as snow; and for fear of Him those fierce, hard soldiers, who feared neither God nor man, shook, and became as dead men. And Christ arose and went forth. How he rose—how he looked when he arose, no man can tell, for no man saw. Only before the sun was risen came Mary Magdalene, and the other Mary, and found the stone rolled away, and saw the angels sitting, clothed in white, who said, "Fear not, for I know that ye seek Jesus, who was crucified. He is not here, for He is risen. Come, see the place where the Lord lay."

What must they have thought, poor, faithful souls, who came, lonely and broken-hearted, to see the place where *He*, their only hope, was, as they thought, shut up and lost for ever, to hear that He was risen and gone? Half terrified, half delighted, they went back with other women who had come on the same errand, with spices to anoint the blessed body, and told the apostles. Peter and John ran to the sepulchre, and saw the linen clothes lie, and the napkin that was about his blessed head, wrapped together by itself. They then believed. Then first broke on them the meaning of His old saying, that He must rise from the dead; and so, wondering and doubting what to do, they went back home.

But Mary—faithful, humble Mary—stood without, by the sepulchre, weeping. The angels called to her, "Woman, why weepest thou?" "They have taken away my Lord," said she; "and I know not where they have laid him."

Then, in a moment, out of the air, He appeared behind her. His body had been changed; it was now a glorified, spiritual body, which could appear and disappear when and how he liked. She turned back, and saw Him standing, but she knew Him not. A wondrous change had come over Him since last she saw Him hanging, bleeding, pale, and dying, on the cross of shame. "Woman," said He, "why weepest thou?" She, fancying it was the gardener, said to Him, "Sir, if thou hast borne Him hence, tell me where thou hast laid Him, and I will take Him away." Jesus said to her, "Mary." At the sound of that beloved voice—His own voice—calling by her name, her recollection came back to her. She knew Him—knew Him for her risen Lord; and, falling at His feet, cried out, "My Master!"

So Jesus Christ, the Son of God, rose from the dead!

Now come the questions, *Why* did Christ rise from the dead?—and *how* did he rise? And, first, I will say a few words about how he rose from the dead. And this the Bible will answer for us, as it will every thing else about the spirit-world. Christ, says the Bible, was put to death in the flesh; but quickened, that is, brought to life, by the Spirit. Now what is the Spirit but the Lord and Giver of Life,—life of all sorts—life to the soul—life to the body—life to the trees and plants around us? With that Spirit Christ is filled infinitely without measure; it is *His* Spirit. He is the Prince of Life; and the Spirit which gives life is His Spirit, proceeding from the Father and the Son. *Therefore* the gates of hell could not prevail against Him—*therefore* the heavy grave-stone could not hold Him down—*therefore* His flesh could not see corruption and decay as other bodies do; not because His body was different from other bodies in its substance, but because *He* was filled, body and soul, with the great Spirit of Life. For this is the great business of the Spirit of God, in all nature, to bring life out of death—new generations out of old. What says David? "When Thou, O God, turnest away Thy face, things die and return again to the dust; when Thou lettest Thy breath (which is the same as Thy spirit) go forth, they are made, and Thou renewest the face of the earth." This is the way that seeds, instead of rotting and perishing, spring up and become new plants—God breathes His spirit on them. The seeds must have heat, and damp, and darkness, and electricity, before they can sprout; but the heat, and damp, and darkness, do not make them sprout; they want something more to do that. A philosopher can find out exactly what a seed is made of, and he might make a seed of the proper materials, and put it in the ground, and electrify it—but would it grow? Not it. To grow it must have life—life from the fountain of life—from God's Spirit. All the philosophers in the world have never yet been able, among all the things which they have made, to make a single living thing—and say they never shall; because, put together all they will, still one thing is wanting—*life*, which God alone can give. Why do I say this? To shew you what God's Spirit is; to put you in mind that it is near you, above you, and beneath you, about your path in your daily walk. And also, to explain to you how Christ rose by that Spirit,—how your bodies, if you claim your share in Christ's Spirit, may rise by it too.

You can see now, how Christ, being filled with God's Spirit, rose of Himself. People had risen from the dead before Christ's time, but they had been either raised in answer to the prayers of holy men who had God's Spirit, or at some peculiar time when heaven was opened, and God chose to alter His laws (as we call it) for a moment.

But here was a Man who rose of Himself. He was raised by God, and therefore He raised Himself, for He was God.

You all know what life and power a man's own spirit will often give him. You may have heard of "spirited" men in great danger, or "spirited" soldiers in battle; when faint, wounded, having suffered enough, apparently, to kill them twice over, still struggling or fighting on, and doing the most desperate deeds to the last, from the strength and courage of their spirits conquering pain and weakness, and keeping off, for a time, death itself. We all know how madmen, diseased in their spirits, will, when the fit is on them, have, for a few minutes, ten men's strength. Well, just think, if a man's own spirit, when it is powerful, can give his body such life and force, what must it have been with Christ, who was filled full of *the* Spirit—God's Spirit, the Lord and Giver of life. The Lord could not *help* rising. All the disease, and poison, and rottenness in the world, could not have made His body decay; mountains on mountains could not have kept it down. His body!—the Prince of Life!—He that was the life itself! It was impossible that death could hold Him.

And does not this shew us *why* He rose, that we might rise with Him? What did He say about His own death? "Except a corn of wheat fall into the ground and die, it abideth alone, but if it die it bringeth forth much fruit." He was the grain which fell into the ground and died, and from His dead body sprung up another body—His glorified body; and we His Church, His people, fed with that body—His members, however strange it may sound—St. Paul said it, and therefore I dare to say it, little as I know what it means—members of His flesh and of His bones.

But think! Remember what St. Paul tells you about this very matter in that glorious chapter which is read in the burial-service, "how when thou sowest seed, thou sowest not that body which it will have, but bare grain; but God gives it a body as it hath pleased Him, and to every seed its own body." For the wheat-plant is in reality the same thing as the wheat-seed, and its life the same life, different as the outside of it may look. Dig it up just at this time of year, and you will find the seed-corn all gone, sucked dry; the life of the wheat-seed has formed it into a wheat-plant—yet it is the same individual thing. The substance of the seed has gone into the root and the young blade; but it is the same individual substance. You know it is, and though you cannot tell why, yet you say "What a fine plant that seed has grown into," because you feel it is so, that the seed is the very same thing as the plant which springs up from it, though its shape is changed, and its size, and its colour, and the very stuff of which it was made is changed, since it was a mere seed. And yet it is at bottom the same individual thing as the seed was, with a new body and shape.

So with Christ's body. It was changed after He rose. It had gone through pain, and weakness, and death, gone down to the lowest depth of them, and conquered them, and passed triumphant through them and far beyond their power. His body was now a nobler, a more beautiful, a glorified body, a spiritual body, one which could do whatever His Spirit chose to make it do, one which could never die again, one which could come through closed doors, appear and vanish as He liked, instead of being bound to walk the earth, and stand cold and heat, sickness and weariness.

Yet it was the very same body, just as the wheat-plant is the same as the wheat-seed—the very same body. Every one knew His face again after His resurrection. There was the very print of the nails to be seen in His hands and feet, the spear-wound in His blessed side. So shall it be with us, my friends. We shall rise again, and we shall be the same as we are now, and yet not the same; our bodies shall be the same bodies, and yet nobler, purer, spiritual bodies, which can know neither death, nor pain, nor weariness. Then, never care, my friends, if we drop like ripe grain into the bosom of mother earth,—if we are to spring up again as seedling plants, after death's long winter, on the resurrection morn. Truly says the poet, [187] how

> "Mother earth, she gathers all
> Into her bosom, great and small:
> Oh could we look into her face,
> We should not shrink from her embrace."

No, indeed! for if we look steadily with the wise, searching eye of faith into the face of mother earth, we shall see how death is but the gate of life, and this narrow churchyard, with its corpses close-packed underneath the sod, would not seem to us a frightful charnel-house of corruption. No! it would seem like what it is—a blessed, quiet, seed-filled God's garden, in which our forefathers, after their long-life labour, lay sown by God's friendly hand, waiting peaceful, one and all, to spring up into leaf, and flower, and everlasting paradise-fruit, beneath the breath of God's Spirit at the last great day, when the Sun of Righteousness arises in glory, and the summer begins which shall never end.

One and all, did I say? Alas! would God it were so! We cannot hope as for all, but they are dead and gone, and we are not here to judge the dead. They have another Judge, and all shall be as He wills.

But we—we in whose limbs the breath of life still boils—we who can still work, let us never forget all grain ripens not. There is some falls out of the ear unripe, and perishes; some is picked out by birds; some withers and decays in the ear, and yet gets into the barn with it, and is sown too with the wheat, of which I never heard that any sprang up again—ploughed up again it may be—a withered, dead husk of chaff as it died, ploughed up to the resurrection of damnation to burn as chaff in unquenchable fire; but the good seed alone, ripe, and safe with the wheat-plant till it is ripe, that only will *spring up* to the resurrection of eternal life.

Now, consider again that parable of the wheat-plant. After it has sprung up, what does it next, but *tiller?*—and every new shoot that tillers out bears its own ear, ripens its own grain, twenty, thirty, or forty stems, and yet they are all the same plant, living with the life of that one original seed. So with Christ's Church—His body the Church. As soon as he rose, that new plant began to tiller. He did not keep His Spirit to Himself, but poured it out on the apostles, and from them it spread and spread—Each generation of Christians ripening, and bearing fruit, and dying, a fresh generation of fruit springing up from them, and so on, as we are now at this day. And yet all these plants, these millions and millions of Christian men and women, who have lived since Christ's blessed resurrection, all are parts of that one original seed, the body of Christ, whose members they are, and all owe their life to that one spirit of Christ, which is in them all and through them all, as the life of the original grain is in the whole crop which springs from it.

And what can you learn from this? Learn this, that in Christ you are safe, out of Christ you are lost. But *really* in Christ, I mean—not like the dead and dying grains, mildewed and worm-eaten, which you find here and there on the finest wheat-plant. Their end is to be burned, and so will ours be, for all our springing out of Christ's root, if the angel reapers find us not good wheat, but chaff and mildew. Every branch in Christ which beareth not fruit, His heavenly Father taketh away. Therefore, never pride yourself on having been baptised into Christ, never pride yourself on shewing some signs of God's Spirit, on being really good, right in this and right in that,—the question is, not so much, Are you *in Christ* at all, are you part of His tree, a member of His body? but, Are you ripening there? If you are not ripening, you are decaying, and your end will be as God has said. And do you wish to know whether you are in Christ, safe, ripening? see whether you are like Him. If the young grain does not shew like the seed grain, you may be sure it is making no progress; and as surely as a wheat-plant never brought forth rye, or a grape-tree thistles, so surely, if you are not like Christ in your character, in patience, in meekness, in courage, truth, purity, piety, and love, you may be of His planting, but you are none of His ripening, and you will not be raised with Him at the last day, to flower anew in the gardens of Paradise, world without end.

SERMON XVIII.
IMPROVEMENT.

Psalm xcii. 12.

"The righteous shall flourish like the palm-tree: he shall grow like the cedar in Lebanon. Those that be planted in the house of the Lord shall flourish in the courts of our God. They shall still bring forth fruit in old age; they shall be fat and flourishing."

The Bible is always telling Christian people to *go forwards*—to grow—to become wiser and stronger, better and better day by day; that they ought to become better, and better, because they can, if they choose, improve. This text tells us so; it says that we shall bring forth more fruit in our old age. Another text tells us that "those who wait on the Lord shall renew their strength;" another tells us that we "shall go from strength to strength." Not one of St. Paul's Epistles but talks of growing in grace and in the knowledge of God, of being *filled* with God's Spirit, of having our eyes more and more open to understand God's truth. Not one of St. Paul's Epistles but contains prayers of St. Paul that the men to whom he writes may become holier and wiser. And St. Paul says that he himself needed to go forward—that he wanted fresh strength—that he had to forget what was past, and consider all he had done and felt as nothing, and press forward to the prize of his high calling; that he needed to be daily conquering himself more and more, keeping down his bad feelings, hunting out one bad habit after another, lest, by any means, when he had preached to others, he himself should become a castaway. Therefore, I said rightly, that the Bible is always bidding us go forwards. You cannot read your Bibles without seeing this. What else was the use of St. Paul's Epistles? They were written to Christian men, redeemed men, converted men, most of them better I fear than ever we shall be; and for what? to tell them not be content to remain as they were, to tell them to go forwards, to improve, to be sure that they were only just inside the gate of God's kingdom, and that if they would go on to perfection, they would find strength, and holiness, and blessing, and honour, and happiness, which they as yet did not dream of. "Be ye perfect, even as your Father which is in heaven is perfect," said our blessed Lord to all men. "Be ye perfect," says St. Paul to the Corinthians, and the Ephesians, and all to whom he wrote; and so say I to you now in God's name, for Christ's sake, as citizens of God's kingdom, as heirs of everlasting glory, "Be you perfect, even as your Father in heaven is perfect."

Now I ask you, my friends, is not this reasonable? It is reasonable, for the Bible always speaks of our souls as living things. It compares them to limbs of a body, to branches of a tree, often to separate plants—as in our Lord's parable of the tares and the wheat. Again, St. Paul tells us that we have been planted in baptism in the likeness of Christ's death; and again, in the first Psalm, which says that the good man shall be like a tree planted by the waterside; and again, in the text of my sermon, which says "that those who are planted in the house of the Lord shall flourish in the courts of our God. They shall still bring forth fruit in old age; they shall be fat and flourishing."

Now what does all this mean? It means that the life of our souls is in some respects like the life of a plant; and, therefore, that as plants grow, so our souls are to grow. Why do you plant anything, but in order that it may *grow* and become larger, stronger, bear flower and fruit? Be sure God has planted us in His garden, Christ's Church, for no other reason. Consider, again— What is life but a continual growing, or a continual decaying? If a tree does not get larger and stronger, year by year, is not that a sure sign that it is unhealthy, and that decay has begun in it, that it is unsound at heart? And what happens then? It begins to become weaker and smaller, and cankered and choked with scurf and moss till it dies. If a tree is not growing, it is sure in the long run to be dying; and so are our souls. If they are not growing they are dying; if they are not getting better they are getting worse. This is why the Bible compares our souls to trees—not out of a mere pretty fancy of poetry, but for a great, awful, deep, world-wide lesson, that every tree in the fields may be a pattern, a warning, to us thoughtless men, that as that tree is meant to grow, so our souls are meant to grow. As that tree dies unless it grows, so our souls must die unless they grow. Consider that!

But how does a tree grow? How are our souls to grow? Now here, again, we shall understand heavenly things best by taking and considering the pattern from among earthly things which the Bible gives us—the tree, I mean. A tree grows in two ways. Its roots take up food from the ground, its leaves take up food from the air. Its roots are its mouth, we may say, and its leaves are its lungs. Thus the tree draws nourishment from the earth beneath and from the heaven above; and so must our souls, my friends, if they are to live and grow, they must have food both from earth and from heaven. And this is what I mean—Why has God given us senses, eyes, and ears, and understanding? That by them we may feed our souls with things which we see and hear, things which are going on in the world round us. We must read, and we must listen, and we must watch people and their sayings and doings, and what becomes of them, and we must try and act, and practise what is right for ourselves; and so we shall, by using our eyes and ears and our bodies, get practice, and experience, and knowledge, from the world round us—such as Solomon gives us in his Proverbs—and so our eyes, and ears, and understandings, are to be to us like roots, by which we may feed our souls with earthly learning and experience. But is this enough? No, surely. Consider, again, God's example which He has given us—a tree. If you keep stripping all the leaves off a tree, as fast as they grow, what becomes of it? It dies, because without leaves it cannot get nourishment from the air, and the rain, and the sunlight. Again, if you shut up a tree where it can get neither rain, air, nor light, what happens? the tree certainly dies, though it may be planted in the very richest soil, and have the very strongest roots; and why? because it can get no food from the sky above. So with our souls, my friends. If we get no food from above, our souls will die, though we have all the wit, and learning, and experience, in the world. We must be fed, and strengthened, and satisfied, with the grace of God from above—with the Spirit of God. Consider how the Bible speaks of God's Spirit as the breath of God; for the very word *spirit* means, originally, breath, or air, or gas, or a breeze of wind, shewing us that as without the airs of heaven the tree would become stunted and cankered, so our souls will without the fresh, purifying breath of God's Spirit. Again, God's Spirit is often spoken of in Scripture as dew and rain. His grace or favour, we read, is as dew on the grass; and again, that God shall come unto us as the rain, as the first and latter rain upon the earth; and again, speaking of the outpourings of God's Spirit on His Church, the Psalmist says that "He shall come down as the rain upon the mown grass, as showers that water the earth;" and to shew us that as the tree puts forth buds, and leaves, and tender wood, when it drinks in the dew and rains, so our hearts will become tender, and bud out into good thoughts and wise resolves, when God's Spirit fills them with His grace.

But again; the Scripture tells us again and again that our souls want light from above; and we all know by experience that the trees and plants which grow on earth want the light of the sun to make them grow. So, doubtless, here again the Scripture example of a tree will hold good. Now what does the sunlight do for the tree? It does every thing, for without light, the soil, and air, and rain, are all useless. It stirs up the sap, it hardens the wood, it brings out the blossom, it colours the leaves and the flowers, it ripens the fruit. The light is the life of the tree;—and is there not one, my friends, of whom these words are written—that He is the Life, and that He is the Light—that He is the Sun of Righteousness and the bright and morning Star—that He is the light which lighteth every man that cometh into the world—that in Him was life, and the life was the light of men? Do you not know of whom I speak? Even of Him that was born at Bethlehem and died on the cross, who now sits at God's right hand, praying for us, offering to us His body and His blood;—Jesus the Son of God, He is the Light and the Life. From Him alone our light must come, from Him alone our life must come, now and for ever. Oh, think seriously of this—and think, too, how a short time before He died on earth He spoke of Himself as the Bread of life—the living Bread which comes down from heaven; how He declared to men, that unless they eat His flesh and drink His blood, they have no life in them. And, lastly, consider this, how the same night that He was betrayed, He took bread, and when He had given thanks, He brake it, and said, "Take, eat; this is my body, which is given for you; this do in remembrance of me." And how, likewise, He took the cup, and when He had blessed it, He gave it to them, saying, "Drink ye all of this, for this is the new covenant in my blood, which is shed for you and for many, for the forgiveness of sins; this do, as oft as ye drink it, in remembrance of me." Oh, consider these words, my friends—to you all and every one they were spoken. "Drink ye *all* of this," said the Blessed One; and will you refuse to drink it? He offers you the bread of life, the sign and the pledge of His body, which shall feed your souls with everlasting strength and life; and will you refuse what the Son of God offers you, what He bought for you with His death? God forbid, my friends! This is your blessed right and privilege—the right and the privilege of every one of you—to come freely and boldly to that holy table, and there to remember your Saviour. At that table to confess your Saviour before men—at that table to shew that you really believe that Jesus Christ died for you—at that table to claim your share in the strength of His body, in the pardon of His blood, which cleanses from all sin—and at that table to receive what you claim, to receive at that table the wine, as a sign from Christ Himself, that His blood has washed away your sins; and the bread, as a sign that His body and His spirit are really feeding your spirits, that your souls are strengthened and refreshed by the body and blood of Christ, as your bodies are with the bread and wine. I have shewn you that your souls must be fed from heaven,—that the Lord's Supper is a sign to you that they *are* fed from heaven. You pray to God, I hope, many of you, that He would give you His Holy Spirit, that He would change, and renew, and strengthen your souls—you pray God to do this, I hope—Well, then, there is the answer to your prayers. There your souls *will* be renewed and strengthened—there you will claim your share in Christ, who alone can renew and strengthen them. The bread which is there broken is the communion, the sharing, of the body of Christ; the cup which is there blessed is the communion of the blood of Christ: to that heavenly treat, to that spiritual food of your souls, Jesus Himself invites you, He who is the life of men. Do not let it be said at the last day of any one of you, that when the Son of God Himself invites you, you would not come to Him that you might have life.

SERMON XIX.
MAN'S WORKING DAY.

JOHN, xi. 9, 10.

"Jesus answered, Are there not twelve hours in the day? If any man walk in the day, he stumbleth not, because he seeth the light of this world. But if a man walk in the night he stumbleth, because there is no light in him."

THIS was our blessed Lord's answer to His disciples when they said to Him, "Master, the Jews of late tried to stone Thee, and goest Thou among them again?" And "Jesus answered, Are there not twelve hours in the day? If any man walk in the day he stumbleth not, because he seeth the light of this world. But if a man walk in the night he stumbleth, because there is no light in him."

Now, at first sight, one does not see what this has to do with the disciples' question—it seems no answer at all to it. But we must remember who it was who gave that answer. The Son of God, from whom all words come, who came to do good, and only good, every minute of His life. And, therefore, we may be sure that He never threw away a single word. And we must remember, too, to whom He spoke—to His disciples, whom He was training to be apostles to the whole world, teaching them in every thing some deep lesson, to fit them for their glorious calling, as preachers of the good news of His coming. So we may be sure that He would never put off any question of theirs; we may be certain, that whatever they asked Him, He would give them the best possible answer; not, perhaps, just the answer for which they wished, but the answer which would teach them most. Therefore I say, we must believe that there is some deep, wonderful lesson in this text—that it is the very best and fullest answer which our Lord could have made to His disciples when they asked Him why He was going again to Judea, where He stood in danger of His life.

Let us think a little about this text in faith, that is, sure that there is a deep, blessed meaning in it, if we can but find it out. Let us take it piece by piece; we shall never get to the bottom of it, of course, but we may get deep enough into it to set us thinking a little between now and next Sunday.

"Are there not twelve hours in the day?" said our Lord. We know there are, and we know, too, that if any man walks in the day, and keeps his eyes open, he does not stumble, because he has the light of this world to guide him. Twelve hours for business, and twelve for food, and sleep, and rest, is our rule for working men, or, indeed, not our rule, but God's. He has set the sun for the light of this world, to rule the day, to settle for us how long we are to work. In this country days vary. In summer they are more than twelve hours, and then men work early and late; but that is made up to us by winter, when the days are less than twelve hours, and men work short time. In the very cold countries again, far away in the frozen north, the sun never sets all the summer, and never rises all the winter, and there is six months day and six months night. Wonderful! But even there God has fitted the land and men's lives to that strange climate, and they can gather in enough meat in the summer to keep them all the winter, that they may be able to spend the long six months' night of winter warm in their houses, sleeping and resting, with plenty of food. So that even to them there are twelve hours in the day, though their hours are each a fortnight long,—I mean a certain fixed time in which to walk, and do the business which they have to do before the long frozen night comes, wherein no man can work, because the sun, the light of this world, is hid from them below the ice for six whole months. So that our Lord's words hold true of all men, even of those people in the icy north. But in by far the most parts of the world, and especially in the hot countries, where our Lord lived, there are twelve common hours in every day, wherein men may and ought to work.

Now what did our Lord mean by reminding His disciples of this, which they all knew already? He meant this,—that God His Father had appointed Him a certain work to do, and a certain time to do it in; that though His day was short, only thirty-three years in all, while we have, many of us, seventy years given us, yet that there were twelve hours in His day in which He must work—that God would take care that He lived out His appointed time, provided He was ready and earnest in doing God's work in it—and that He *must* work in that time which God had given Him, whatever came of it, and do His appointed work before the night of death came in which no man can work.

There was a heathen king once, named Philip of Macedon, and a very wise king he was, though he was a heathen, and one of the wisest of his plans was this:—he had a slave, whom he ordered to come in to him every morning of his life, whatever he was doing, and say to him in a loud voice, "Philip, remember that thou must die!"

He was a heathen, but a great many who call themselves Christians are not half so wise as he, for they take all possible care, not to remember that they must die, but to *forget* that they must die; and yet every living man has a servant who, like King Philip's, puts him in mind, whether he likes it or not, that his day will run out at last, and his twelve hours of life be over, and then die he must. And who is that servant? A man's own body. Lucky if his body is his servant, though—not his *master* and his tyrant. But still, be that as it may, every finger-ache that one's body has, every cough and cold one's body catches, ought to be to us a warning like King Philip's servant, "Remember that thou must die." Every little pain and illness is a warning, a kindly hint from our Father in heaven, that we are doomed to death; that we have but twelve hours in this short day of life, and that the twelve must end; and that we must get our work done and our accounts settled, and be ready for our long journey, to meet our Father and our King, before the night comes wherein no man can work, but only takes his wages; for them who have done good the wages of life eternal, and for them who have done evil—God help them! we know what is written—"the wages of sin is death!"

Now, observe next, that those who walk in the day do not stumble, because they see the light of this world, and those who walk in the night stumble—they have no light in them. If they are to see, it must be by the help of some light outside themselves, which is not part of themselves, or belonging to themselves at all. We only see by the light which God has made; when that is gone, our eyes are useless.

So it is with our souls. Our wits, however clever they may be, only understand things by the light which God throws on those things. He must explain and enlighten all things to us. Without His light—His Spirit, all the wit in the world is as useless as a pair of eyes in a dark night.

Now this earthly world which we do see is an exact picture and pattern of the spiritual, heavenly world which we do not see, as Solomon says in the Proverbs, "The things which are seen are the doubles of the things which are not seen." And as there is a light for us in this earth, which is *not ourselves*, namely the sun, so there is a light for us in the spirit-world, which is *not ourselves*. And who is that? The blessed Lord shall answer for Himself. He says, "I am the light of the world;" and St. John bears witness to Him, "In Him was life, and the life was the light of men." And does not St. Paul say the same thing, when he blessed God so often for having called him and his congregations out of darkness into that marvellous light? If you read his Epistles you will find what he meant by the darkness, what he meant by the light. The darkness was heathendom, knowing nothing of Christ. The light was Christianity, knowing Christ the light; and, more, being *in* the light, belonging to Christ—being joined to Him, as the leaves are to the tree,—living by trust in Christ, being taught and made true men and true women of, by the Noble and Holy Spirit of Christ—seeing their way through this world by trust in Christ and His promises,—That was light.

And there is no other light. If a man does not work trusting in Christ, whom God has set for the light of the world, he works in the night, where God never set or meant him to work; and stumble he will, and make a fool of himself, sooner or later, because he is walking in the night, and sees nothing plainly or in a right view. For as our Lord says truly, "There is no light in him." No light in him? In one sense there is no light in any one, be he the wisest or holiest man who ever lived. But this is just what three people out of four will not believe. They will not believe that the Spirit of God gives man understanding. They fancy that they have light in themselves. They try, conceitedly and godlessly, to walk by the light of their own eyes—to make their own way plain before their face for themselves. They will not believe old David, a man who worked, and fought, and thought, and saw, far more than any one of us will ever do, when he tells them again and again in his Psalms, that the Lord is his light, that the Lord must guide a man, and inform him with His eye, and teach him in the way in which he should go. And, therefore, they will not pray to God for light—therefore they will not look for light in God's Word, and in the writings of godly men; and they are like a man in the broad sunshine, who should choose to shut his eyes close, and say, 'I have light enough in my own head to do without the sun;' and therefore they walk on still in darkness, and all the foundations of the earth are out of course, because men forget the first universal ground rules of common sense, and reason, and love, which God's Spirit teaches. I tell you, all the mistakes that you ever made—that ever were made since Adam fell, came from this, that men will not ask God for light and wisdom; they love darkness rather than light, and therefore, though God's light is ready for every man, shining in the darkness to shew every man his way, yet the darkness will not comprehend it—will not take it in, and let God change its blindness into day.

Now, then, to gather all together, what better answer could our Lord have given to His disciples' question than this, "Are there not twelve hours in the day? If a man walk in the day he does not stumble, because he seeth the light of this world; but if a man walk in the night, he stumbleth, because there is no light in him."

It was as if He had said, "However short my day of life may be, there are twelve hours in it, of my Father's numbering and measuring, not of mine. My times are in His hand, as long as He pleases I shall live. He has given me a work to do, and He will see that I live long enough to do it. Into His hands I commend my spirit, for, living or dying, He is with me. Though I walk through the valley of the shadow of death, He will be with me. He will keep me secretly in His tabernacle from the strife of tongues, and will turn the furiousness of my enemies to His glory; and as my day my strength will be. And I have no fear of running into danger needlessly. I have prayed to Him daily and nightly for light, for His Spirit—the spirit of wisdom and understanding, of prudence and courage; and His word is pledged to keep me in all my ways, so that I dash not my foot against a stone. Know ye not that I must be about my Father's business? While I am about that I am safe. It is only if I go about my own business—my own pleasure; if I forget to ask Him for His light and guidance, that I shall put myself into the night, and stumble and fall."

Well, my friends, what is there in all this, which we may not say as well as our Lord? In this, as in all things, Christ set Himself up as our pattern. Oh, believe it!—believe that your time—your measure of life, is in God's hand. Believe that He is your light, that He will teach and guide you into all truth, and that all your mistakes come from not asking counsel of Him in prayer, and thought, and reading of His Holy Bible. Believe His blessed promise that He will give His Holy Spirit to those who ask Him. Believe, too, that He has given you a work to do—prepared good works all ready for you to walk in. Be you labourer or gentleman, maid, wife, or widow, God has given you a work to do; there is good to be done lying all round you, ready for you. And the blessed Jesus who bought you, body and soul, with His own blood, commands you to work for Him: "Whatsoever your hand finds to do, do it with all your might."

> "Work ye manful while ye may,
> Work for God in this your day;
> Night must stop you, rich or poor,
> Godly deeds alone endure."

And then, whether you live or die, your Father's smile will be on you, and His everlasting arms beneath you, and at your last hour you shall find that "Blessed are the dead that die in the Lord, for they rest from their labour, and their works do follow them."

SERMON XX.
ASSOCIATION.

Galatians, vi. 2.

"Bear ye one another's burdens, and so fulfil the law of Christ."

If I were to ask you, my friends, why you were met together here to-day, you would tell me, I suppose, that you were come to church as members of a benefit club; and quite right you are in coming here as such, and God grant that we may meet together here on this same errand many more Whit-mondays. But this would be no answer to my question; I wish to know why you come to church to-day sooner than to any other place? what has the church to do with the benefit club? Now this is a question which I do not think all of you could answer very readily, and therefore I wish to make you, especially the younger members of the club, think a little seriously about the meaning of your coming here to-day. You will be none the less cheerful this evening for having had some deep and godly thoughts in your heads this morning.

Now these benefit clubs are also called provident societies, and a very good name for them. You become members of them, because you are prudent, or provident, that is, because you are careful, and look forward to a rainy day. But why does not each of you lay up his savings for himself, instead of putting them into a common purse, and so forming a club? Because you have found out, what every one else in the world, but madmen, ought to have found out, that two are better than one; that if a great many men join together in any matter, they are a great deal stronger when working together, than if they each worked just as hard, but each by himself; that the way to be safe is not to stand each of you alone, but to help each other; in short, that there is no getting on without bearing one another's burdens.

Now this plan of bearing one another's burdens is not only good in benefit clubs—it is good in families, in parishes, in nations, in the church of God, which is the elect of all mankind. Unless men hold together, and help each other, there is no safety for them.

Let us consider what there is bearing on this matter of prudence, that makes one of the greatest differences between a man and a brute beast. It is not that the man is prudent, and the beast is not. Many beasts have forethought enough; the very sleepmouse hoards up acorns against the winter; a fox will hide the game he cannot eat. No, the great difference between man and beast is, that the beast has forethought only for himself, but the man has forethought for others also; beasts have not reason enough to bear each others' burdens, as men have. And what is it that makes us call the ant and the bee the wisest of animals, except that they do, in some degree, behave like men, in helping one another, and having some sort of family feeling, and society, and government among them, by which they can help bear each other's burdens? So that we all confess, by calling them wise, how wise it is to help each other. Consider a family, again. In order that a family may be happy and prosperous, all the members of it must bear each other's burdens. If the father only thought of himself, and the mother of herself, and each of the children did nothing but take care of themselves, would not that family come to misery and ruin? But if they all helped each other—all thought of each other more than of themselves—all were ready to give up their own comfort to make each other comfortable, that family would be peaceful and prosperous, and would be doing a great deal towards fulfilling the law of Christ.

It is just the same in a parish. If the rich help and defend the poor, and the poor respect and love the rich, and are ready to serve them as far as they can,—in short, if all ranks bear each other's burdens, that parish is a happy one, and if they do not, it is a miserable one.

Just the same with a nation. If the king only cares about making himself strong, and the noblemen and gentlemen about their rank and riches, and the poor people, again, only care for themselves, and are trying to pull down the rich, and so get what they can for themselves,—if a country is in this state, what can be more wretched? Neither a house, nor a country, divided against itself, can ever stand. But if the king and the nobles give their whole minds to making good laws, and seeing justice done to all, and workmen fairly paid, and if the poor, in their turns, are loyal, and ready to fight and work for their king and their nobles, then will not that country be a happy and a great country? Surely it will, because its people, instead of caring every man for himself only, help each other and bear one another's burdens.

And just in the same way with Christ's Church, with the company of true Christian men. If the clergymen thought only of themselves, and neglected the people, and forgot to labour among them, and pray for them, and preach to them; and if the people each cared for himself, and never prayed to God to give them a spirit of love and charity, and never helped their neighbours, or did unto others as they wished to be done by; and above all, if Christ, our Head, left His Church, and cared no more about us, what would become of Christ's Church? What would happen to the whole race of sinful man, but misery in this world, and ruin in the next? But if the people love and help each other, and obey their ministers, and pray for them; and if the ministers labour earnestly after the souls and bodies of their people; and Christ in heaven helps both minister and people with His Spirit, and His providence and protection; in short, if all in the whole Church bear each other's burdens, then Christ's Church will stand, and the gates of hell will not prevail against it.

Thus you see that this text of bearing one another's burdens is no new or strange commandment, but the very state in which every man is meant to live, both in his family, his parish, his country, and his Church—all his life helping others, and being helped by them in turn. And because families and nations, and the Church of Christ above all, are good, and holy, and beautiful, therefore any society which is formed upon the same plan—I mean of helping each other—must be good also. And, therefore, benefit societies are right and reasonable things, and among all the good which they do they do this one great good, that they teach men to remember that there is no use trying to stand alone, but that the way to be safe and happy is to bear each other's burdens.

Thus benefit societies are patterns of Christ's Church. But now, my friends, there is another point for each of you to consider, which is this—the benefit club is a good thing, but are you a good member of the club? Do you do your duty, each of you, in the club as Christian men should?

I do not ask whether you pay your subscriptions regularly or not—that is quite right and necessary, but there is something more than that wanted to make a club go on rightly. Mere paying and receiving money will never keep men together any more than any other outward business. A man may pay his club-money regularly and yet not be a really good member. And how is this? You remember that I tried to shew you that a family, and a nation, and a church, all were kept together by the same principle of bearing one another's burdens, just as a benefit club is. Now, what makes a man a good member of Christ's Church,—a good Christian, in short? A man may pay his tithes to the rector, and his church-rates to repair God's house, and his poor-rates to maintain God's poor, all very regularly, and yet be a very bad member of Christ's Church. These payments are all right and good; but they are but the outside, the letter of what God requires of him. What is wanted is, to serve God in the *spirit*, to have the spirit—*the will*, of a Christian in him; that is, to do all these things for *God's* sake—not of constraint, but willingly— "not grudgingly, for God loveth a cheerful giver." No! If a man is a really good member of Christ's Church, he lives a life of faith in Jesus Christ, and of thankfulness to Him for His infinite love and mercy in coming down to die for us, and thus the love of God and man is shed abroad in his heart by God's Spirit, which is given to him. Therefore, that man thinks it an honour to pay church-rates, and so help towards keeping God's house in repair and neatness. He pays his tithes cheerfully, because he loves God's ministers, and feels their use and worth to him. He pays his poor-rates with a willing mind, for the sake of that God who has said, "that he who gives to the poor lends to the Lord." And so he obeys not only the letter but the spirit of the law.

But the man does more than this. Besides obeying not only the letter but the spirit of the law, he helps his brethren in a thousand other ways. He shews, in short, by every action that he believes in God and loves his neighbour.

And why should it not be just the same in a benefit club? There the good member is *not* the man who pays his money merely to have a claim for relief when he himself is sick, and yet grudges every farthing that goes to help other members. That man is not a good member. He has come into the club merely to take care of himself, and not to bear others' burdens. He may obey the letter of the club-rules by paying in his subscriptions and by granting relief to sick members, but he does not obey the spirit of them. If he did, he would be glad to bear his sick neighbour's burden with so little trouble to himself. He would, therefore, grant club relief willingly and cheerfully when it was wanted,—ay, he would thank God that he had an opportunity of helping his neighbours. He would feel that all the members of the society were his brothers in a double sense; first, because they had joined with him to help and support each other in the society; and, next, that they were his brothers in Christ, who had been baptised into the same Church of God with himself. And he would, therefore, delight in supporting them in their sickness, and honouring them when they died, and in helping their widows and orphans in their affliction; in short, in bearing his neighbour's burdens, and so fulfilling the law of Christ. And do you not see, that if any of you subscribe to this benefit society in such a spirit as this, that they are the men to give an answer to the question I asked at first, "Why are you all here at church to-day?" They come here for the same reason that you all ought to come, to thank God for having kept them well, and out of the want of relief for the past year, and to thank Him, too, for having enabled them to bear their sick neighbours' burdens. And they come, also, to pray to God to keep them well and strong for the year to come, and to raise up those members who are in sickness and distress, that they may all worship God here together another year, as a company of faithful friends, helping each other on through this life, and all on the way to the same heavenly home, where there will be no more poverty, nor sorrow, nor sickness, nor death, and God shall wipe away tears from all widows and orphans' eyes.

And now, my friends, I have tried to put some new and true thoughts into your head about your club and your business in this church to-day. And I pray, God grant that you may remember them, and think of this whole matter as a much more solemn and holy one than you ever did before.

SERMON XXI.
HEAVEN ON EARTH.

1 COR. x. 31.

"Whether ye eat, or drink, or whatsoever ye do, do all to the glory of God."

THIS is a command from God, my friends, which well worth a few minutes' consideration this day;—well worth considering, because, though it was spoken eighteen hundred years ago, yet God has not changed since that time;—He is just as glorious as ever; and Christian men's relation to God has not changed since that time; they still live, and move, and have their being in God; they are still His children—His beloved; Christ, who died for us, is still our King; God's Spirit is still with us, God's mercy still saves us: we owe God as much as any people ever did. If it was ever any one's duty to shew forth God's glory, surely it is our duty too.

Worth considering, indeed, is this command, for though it is in the Bible, and has been there for eighteen hundred years, it is seldom read, seldomer understood, and still more seldom put into practice. Men eat and drink, and do all manner of things, with all their might and main; but how many of them do they do to the glory of God? No; this is the fault—the especial curse of our day, that religion does not mean any longer, as it used, the service of God—the being like God, and shewing forth God's glory. No; religion means, nowadays, the art of getting to heaven when we die, and saving our own miserable, worthless souls, and getting God's wages without doing God's work—as if that was godliness,—as if that was any thing but selfishness; as if selfishness was any the better for being everlasting selfishness! If selfishness is evil, my friends, the sooner we get rid of it the better, instead of mixing it up as we do with all our thoughts of heaven, and making our own enjoyment and our own safety the vile root of our hopes for all eternity. And therefore it is that people have forgotten what God's glory is. They seem to think, that God's highest glory is saving them from hell-fire. And they talk not of God and of the wondrous majesty of God, but only of the wonder of God's having saved them—looking at themselves all the time, and not at God. We must get rid of this sort of religion, my friends, at all risks, in order to get rid of all sorts of irreligion, for one is the father of the other.

It is a wonder, indeed, that we are saved from hell, much more raised to heaven, such peevish, cowardly, pitiful creatures as the best of us are: and yet the more we think of it, the less wonder we shall find it. The more we think of the wonder of all wonders,—God Himself, His majesty, His power, His wisdom, His love, His pity, His infinite condescension, the less reason we shall have to be surprised that He has stooped to save us. Yes, do not be startled—for it is true, that He has done for sinful men nothing contrary to Himself, but just what was to be expected from such unutterable condescension, and pity, and generosity, as God's is. And so recollecting this, we shall begin to forget ourselves, and look at God; and in thinking of Him we shall get beyond mere wondering at Him, and rise to something higher—to worshipping Him.

Yes, my friends, this is what we must try at if we would be really godly—to find out what God is—to find out His likeness, His character, as He is: and has He not shewn us what He is? He who has earnestly read Christ's story—he who has understood, and admired, and loved Christ's character, and its nobleness and beauty—he who can believe that Jesus Christ is now, at this minute, raising up his heart to good, guiding his thoughts to good, he has seen God; for he has seen the Son, who is the exact likeness of the Father's glory, in whom dwells all the fulness of the Godhead in a bodily shape. Remember, he who knows Christ knows God,—and that knowledge will help us up a noble step farther—it will help us to shew forth God's glory. For when we once know what God's glory is, we shall see how to make others know it too. We shall know how to *do God justice*, to set men right as to their notions of God, to give them, at all events, in our own lives and characters, a pattern of Christ, who is the Pattern of God; and whatsoever we do we shall be able to do all to God's glory.

For what is doing every thing to the glory of God? It is this;—we have seen what God's glory is: He is His own glory. As you say of any very excellent man, you have but to know him to honour him; or of any very beautiful woman, you have but to see her to love her; so I say of God, men have but to see and know Him to love and honour Him.

Well, then, my friends, if we call ourselves Christian men, if we believe that God is our Father, and delight, as on the grounds of common feeling we ought, to honour our Father, we should try to make every one honour Him as He deserves. In short, whatever we do we should make it tend to His glory—make it a lesson to our neighbours, our friends, and our families. We should preach God's glory to them day by day, not by *words* only, often not by words at all, but by our conduct. Ay, there is the secret.—If you wish other men to believe a thing, just behave as if you believed it yourself. Nothing is so infectious as example. If you wish your neighbours to see what Jesus Christ is like, let them see what He can make *you* like. If you wish them to know how God's love is ready to save them from their sins, let them see His love save *you* from *your* sins. If you wish them to see God's tender care in every blessing and every sorrow they have, why let them see you thanking God for every sorrow and every blessing you have. I tell you, friends, example is every thing. One good man,—one man who does not put his religion on once a-week with his Sunday coat, but wears it for his working dress, and lets the thought of God grow into him, and through and through him, till every thing he says and does becomes religious, that man is worth a ton of sermons—he is a living Gospel—he comes in the spirit and power of Elias—he is the image of God. And men see his good works, and admire them in spite of themselves, and see that they are Godlike, and that God's grace is no dream, but that the Holy Spirit is still among men, and that all nobleness and manliness is His gift, His stamp, His picture; and so they get a glimpse of God again in His saints and heroes, and glorify their Father who is in heaven.

Would not such a life be a heavenly life? Ay, it would be more, it would be heaven—heaven on earth: not in versemongering cant, but really. We should then be sitting, as St. Paul tells us, in heavenly places with Jesus Christ, and having our conversation in heaven. All the while we were doing our daily work, following our business, or serving our country, or sitting at our own firesides with wife and child, we should be all that time in heaven. Why not? we are in heaven now—if we had but faith to see it. Oh, get rid of those carnal, heathen notions about heaven, which tempt men to fancy that, after having misused this place—God's earth—for a whole life, they are to fly away when they die, like swallows in autumn, to another place—they know not where—where they are to be very happy—they know not why or how, nor do I know either. Heaven is not a mere *place*, my friends. All places are heaven, if you will be heavenly in them. Heaven is where God is and Christ is. And hell is where God is not and Christ is not. The Bible says, no doubt, there is a place now—somewhere beyond the skies—where Christ especially shews forth His glory—a heaven of heavens: and for reasons which I cannot explain, there must be such a place. But, at all events, here is heaven; for Christ is here and God is here, if we will open our eyes and see them. And how?—How? Did not Christ Himself say, 'If a man will love Me, My Father will love him; and we, My Father and I, will come to him, and make our abode with him, and we will shew ourselves to him?' Do those words mean nothing or something? If they have any meaning, do they not mean this, that in this life, we can see God—in this life we can have God and Christ abiding with us? And is not that heaven? Yes, heaven is where God is. You are in heaven if God is with you, you are in hell if God is not with you; for where God is not, darkness and a devil are sure to be.

There was a great poet once—Dante by name—who described most truly and wonderfully, in his own way, heaven and hell, for, indeed, he had been in both. He had known sin and shame, and doubt and darkness and despair, which is hell. And after long years of misery, he had got to know love and hope, and holiness and nobleness, and the love of Christ and the peace of God, which is heaven. And so well did he speak of them, that the ignorant people used to point after him with awe in the streets, and whisper, There is the man who has been in hell. Whereon some one made these lines on him:—

> "Thou hast seen hell and heaven? Why not? since heaven and hell
> Within the struggling soul of every mortal dwell."

Think of that!—thou—and thou—and thou!—for in thee, at this moment, is either heaven or hell: and which of them? Ask thyself—ask thyself, friend. If thou art not in heaven in this life, thou wilt never be in heaven in the life to come. At death, says the wise man, each thing returns into its own element, into the ground of its life; the light into the light, and the darkness into the darkness. As the tree falls so it lies. My friends, who call yourselves enlightened Christian folk, do you suppose that you can lead a mean, worldly, covetous, spiteful life here, and then the moment your soul leaves the body that you are to be changed into the very opposite character, into angels and saints, as fairy tales tell of beasts changed into men? If a beast can be changed into a man, then death can change the sinner into a saint,—but not else. If a beast would enjoy being a man, then a sinner would enjoy being in heaven, but not else. A sinful, worldly man enjoy being in heaven? Does a fish enjoy being on dry land? The sinner would long to be back in this world again. Why, what is the employment of spirits in heaven, according to the Bible (for that is the point to which I have been trying to lead you round again)? What but glorifying God? Not *trying* only to do every thing to God's glory, but actually succeeding in *doing* it—basking in the sunshine of His smile, delighting to feel themselves as nothing before His glorious majesty, meditating on the beauty of His love, filling themselves with the sight of His power, searching out the treasures of His wisdom, and finding God in all and all in God—their whole eternity one act of worship, one hymn of praise. Are there not some among us who will have had but little practice at that work? Those who have done nothing for God's glory here, how do they expect to be able to do every thing for God's glory hereafter? (Those who will not take the trouble of merely standing up at the psalms, like the rest of their neighbours, even if they cannot sing with their voices God's praises in this church, how will they like singing God's praises through eternity?) No; be sure that the only people who will be fit for heaven, who will like heaven even, are those who have been in heaven in this life,—the only people who will be able to do every thing to God's glory in the new heavens and new earth, are those who have been trying honestly to do all to His glory in this heaven and this earth.

Think over, in the meantime, what I have said this day; consider it, and you will have enough to think of, and pray over too, till we meet here again.

SERMON XXII.
NATIONAL PRIVILEGES.

LUKE, x. 23.

"Blessed are the eyes which see the things which ye see: for I tell you, that many prophets and kings have desired to see those things which ye see, and have not seen them; and to hear those things which ye hear, and have not heard them."

THIS is a noble text, my friends—and yet an awful one, for if it does not increase our religion, it will certainly increase our condemnation. It tells us that we, even the meanest among us, are more favoured by God than the kings, and judges, and conquerors of the old world, of whom we read this afternoon in the first lesson; that we have more light and knowledge of God than even the prophets David, Isaiah, Jeremiah, and Ezekiel, to whom God's glory appeared in visible shape. It tells us that we see things which they longed to see, and could not; that words are spoken to us for which their ears longed in vain; that they, though they died in hope, yet received not the promises, God having provided some better things for us, that they without us should not be made perfect.

Now, what was this which they longed for, and had not, and yet we have? It was this,—a Saviour and a Saviour's kingdom. All wise and holy hearts for ages—as well heathens as Jews—had had this longing. They wanted a Saviour,—one who should free them from sin and conquer evil,—one who should explain to them all the doubt and contradiction and misery of the world, and give them some means of being freed from it,—one who should set them the perfect pattern of what a man should be, and join earth and heaven, and make godliness part of man's daily life. They longed for a Saviour, and for a heavenly kingdom also. They saw that all the laws in the world could never make men good; that one half of men broke them, and the other half only obeyed them unwillingly through slavish fear, loving the sin they dared not do. That men got worse and worse as time rolled on. That kings, instead of being shepherds of their people, were only wolves and tyrants to keep them in ignorance and misery. That priests only taught the people lies, and fattened themselves at their expense. That, in short, as David said, men would not learn, or understand, and all the foundations of the earth, the grounds and principles of society, politics and religion, were out of course, and the devil very truly the king of this lower world; so they longed for a heavenly kingdom—a kingdom of God, one in which men should obey God for love, and not for fear, and man for God's sake; a spiritual kingdom—a kingdom whose laws should be written in men's hearts and spirits, and be their delight and glory, not their dread. They longed for a

King of kings, who should teach all kings and magistrates to rule in love and wisdom. They longed for a High-priest, who should teach all priests to explain the wonder and the glory that there is in every living man, and in heaven and earth, and all that therein lies, and lead men's hearts into love, and purity, and noble thoughts and deeds. They longed, in short, for a kingdom of God, a golden age, a regeneration of the world, as they called it, and rightly. Of course, the Jewish prophets saw most clearly how this would be brought about, and how utterly necessary a Saviour and His kingdom was to save mankind from utter ruin. They, I say, saw this best. But still all the wise and pious heathens, each according to his measure of light, saw the same necessity, or else were restless and miserable, because they could not see it. So that in all ages of the world, in a thousand different shapes, there was rising up to heaven a mournful, earnest prayer,—"Thy kingdom come!"

And now this kingdom is come, and the King of it, the Saviour of men, is Jesus Christ, the Son of God. Long men prayed, and long men waited, and at last, in the fulness of God's good time, just when the night seemed darkest, and under the abominations of the Roman Empire, religion, honesty, and common decency, seemed to have died out, the Sun of Righteousness rose on the dead and rotten world, to bring life and immortality to light. God sent forth His Son made of a woman, not to condemn the world, but that the world, through Him, might be saved. He sent Him to be our Saviour, to die on the cross for our sins and our children's, that all our guilt might be washed away, and we might come boldly to the throne of grace, with our hearts sprinkled from an evil conscience, and our bodies washed in the waters of baptism. He sent Him to be our Teacher in the perfect law of love, our pattern in every thing which a man should be, and is not. He sent Him to conquer death by rising from the dead, that He might have power to raise us also to life and immortality. He sent Him to fill men with His Spirit, the Spirit of reason and truth, the Spirit of love and courage, that he might know the will of God, and do it as our Saviour did before us. He sent Him to found a Church, to join all men into one brotherhood, one kingdom of God, whose rulers are kings and parliaments, whose ministers are the clergy, whose prophets are all poets and philosophers, authors and preachers, who are true to their own calling; whose signs and tokens are the sacraments; a kingdom which should never be moved, but should go on for ever, drawing into all honest and true hearts, and preserving them ever for Christ their Lord.

And that we might not doubt that we, too, belonged to this kingdom, He has placed in this land His ministers and teachers, Christ's sacraments, Christ's churches in every parish in the land, Christ's Bible, or the means of attaining the Bible, in every house and every cottage; that from our cradle to our grave we might see that we belonged, as sworn servants and faithful children, to the great Father in heaven and Jesus Christ, the King of the earth.

Thus, my friends, all that all men have longed for we possess; we want no more, and we shall have no more. If, under the present state of things, we cannot be holy, we shall never be holy. If we cannot use our right in this kingdom of Christ, how can we become citizens of God's everlasting kingdom, when Christ shall have delivered up the dominion to His Father, and God shall be all in all? God has done all for us that God will do. He has given us His Son for a Saviour, and a Church in which and by which to worship that Saviour; and what more would we have? Alas! my friends, have we yet used fairly what God has given us? and if not, how terrible will be our guilt! "How shall we escape if we neglect so great salvation?" And yet how many do neglect—how few live as if they were citizens of Christ's kingdom! It seems as if God had been too good to us, and heaped us so heavily with blessings, that we were tired of them, and despised them as common things. Common things? They are the very things, as I said, which the great and the wise in all ages have longed for and prayed for, and yet never found! Surely, surely, God may well say to us, "What could have been done unto my vineyard which has not been done to it?" What, indeed? I wish I could take some of you into a heathen country for a single week, that you might see what it is not to know of a Saviour—not to be members of His Church, as we are. Why, we here in England are in the very garden of the Lord. We have but to stretch out our hand to the tree of life, and eat and live for ever. From our cradle to our grave, Christ the King is ready to guide, to teach, to comfort, to deliver us. When we are born, we are christened in His name, made members of Christ, children of God, and inheritors by hope of the kingdom of heaven. Is that nothing? It is, alas! nothing in the eyes of most parents! As we grow older, are we not taught who we are—taught call God our Father—taught about Jesus Christ, who He is, and what He is? Is that, too, nothing? Alas! that knowledge is generally a mere meaningless school-lesson, cared for neither by child nor by man. At confirmation, again, we solemnly declare that we belong to Christ's kingdom, and that we will live as His subjects, and His alone. And we are brought to His bishops, to be received as free, reasonable, Christian people, to claim our citizenship in the kingdom of God. Is that nothing? Yet that, too, is nothing with three-fourths of us. Nothing? Hear me, young people—as I have often told you—you are ready enough to excuse yourselves from your confirmation vows, by saying you were not taught to understand them—were not taught how to put them into practice. That may be true, or it may not; your sin is just the same. No one with any common honesty or common sense could answer as you have to the bishop's questions at confirmation, without knowing that you did make a promise, and knowing well enough what you promised—and you who carried to confirmation a careless heart and a lying tongue, have only yourselves to blame for it!—But to proceed. Is not Christ present, or ready to be present, with us? Sunday after Sunday, for years, have not the churches been opened all around us, inviting us to enter and worship Christ, knowing that where two or three are gathered together, there is Christ in the midst of them. Is that nothing? This Creed—these Lessons—these prayers, which Sunday after Sunday you have used;—are they nothing? Are they not all proofs that the kingdom of God is come to you, and means whereby you can behave like children of the kingdom? And not on Sundays alone. Have we not been taught daily, in our own houses, in our own hearts, in all danger, and trouble, and temptation, to pray to Jesus Christ, our King, knowing that He will hear and save all them that put their trust in Him?

Is that nothing? On our happy marriage morn, too, was it not in God's house, before Christ's minister, in Christ's name, that we were married? Surely the kingdom of God is come to us, when our wedlock, as well as our souls and bodies, is holy to the Lord. Is that nothing? How few think of their marriage-joys as holy things—an ordinance of Christ's kingdom, which He delights in and blesses with His presence and His special smile, seeing that it is the noblest and the purest of all things on earth—the picture of the great mystery which shall be the bridal of all bridals, the marriage of Christ and His Church! People do not, nowadays, believe in marriage as a part of their religion; and so, according to their want of faith it happens to them; their marriage is not holy, and the love and joy of their youth wither into a peevish, careless, lonely old age;—and yet over their heads these words were said, "They are man and wife together, in the Name of the Father, and of the Son, and of the Holy Ghost!" comes of not believing in Christ's presence and Christ's favour; of not believing, in short, in what the Creed truly calls the Holy Catholic Church. Neither after that does Christ leave us. Every time a woman is churched, is not that meant to be a sign of thankfulness to Christ, the great Physician, to whom she owes her life and health once more? Then, season after season, is the sacrament of Christ's body and blood offered you. Is that no sign that Christ is here among us? Ah! blessed are the eyes which see that—blessed are the ears which hear those words, "Take, eat; this is My body which is given for you." Truly, if that honour—that blessing—is so vast, the love and the condescension of Christ, the Lamb of God, so unutterable, that prophets and kings, whatever they believed, never could have desired, never could have imagined, that the Son of God should offer to the sons of men, year after year, in their little parish churches, His most precious body, His most precious blood. And another thing, too, those prophets and kings would never have imagined,—that when Christ, in those churches, offers His body and His blood, nine-tenths of the congregation, calling themselves Christians, should quietly walk out, and go home, and leave the sacraments of Christ's body and Christ's blood behind as a useless and unnecessary matter! That, indeed, the old prophets and kings never saw, and never expected to see—but so it is. Christ is among us, and our eyes are holden, and we know Him not.

And then at last, after all these blessed privileges, these tokens of God's kingdom have been neglected through a long life, does Christ neglect us in the hour of death? Ah, no! He is at the grave, as He was at the font, at the marriage-bed, at His own holy table in God's house; and the body is laid in the ground by Christ's minister, in the certain hope of a joyful resurrection. But what—a sure and certain hope for each and all? The resurrection is a joyful hope—but is it so for all? Only, too often, a faint, dim longing that clings to the last chance, and dares not confess to itself how hopeless must be the death of that man or woman whose life was spent in the kingdom of God, in the midst of blessings which kings said prophets desired in vain to see, and yet who neglected them all, never entered into the spirit of them—never loved them—never lived according to them, but despised and trampled under foot the kingdom of God from their childhood to their grave, as three-fourths of us do. Christ came to judge no man, and therefore Christ's ministers judge no man, and read the Christian funeral service over all, and pray Christ to be there, and to remember His blessed promise of raising up the body and soul to everlasting life. But how can they help fearing that Christ will not hear them—that after all His offers and gifts in this life have been despised, He will give nothing after death but death; and that it were better for the sinful, worldly sham Christian, when lying in his coffin, if he had never been born? How can those escape who neglect such great salvation?

Ah, my friends—my friends, take this to heart! Blessed, indeed, are the eyes which see what you see, and hear what you hear; prophets and kings have desired to see and hear them, and have not seen or heard! But if you, cradled among all these despised honours and means of grace, bring forth no fruit in your lives—shut out from yourselves the thought of your high calling in Jesus Christ; what shall be your end but ruin? He that despises Christ, Christ will despise him; and say not to yourselves, as many do, We are church-goers—we are all safe. I say to you, God is able, from among the Negro and the wild Irishman—ay, God is able of these stones to raise up children to the Church of England, while those of you, the children of the kingdom, who lived in the Church of your fathers, and never used or loved her, or Christ, her King, shall be cast into outer darkness, where there shall be weeping and gnashing of teeth.

SERMON XXIII.
LENTEN THOUGHTS.

HAGGAI, i. 5.

"Now, therefore, thus saith the Lord of Hosts, consider your ways."

NEXT Wednesday is Ash-Wednesday, the first day of Lent, the season which our forefathers have appointed for us to consider and mend our ways, and return, year by year, heart and soul to that Lord and Heavenly Father from whom we are daily wandering. Now, we all know that we ought to have repented long ago; we all know that, sinning in many things daily, as we do, we ought all to repent daily. But that is not enough; we do want, unless we are wonderfully better than the holy men of old,—we do want, I say, a particular time in which we may sit down deliberately and look our own souls steadily in the face, and cast up our accounts with God, and be thoroughly ashamed and terrified at those accounts when we find, as we shall, that we cannot answer God one thing in a thousand. It is all very well to say, I confess and repent of my sins daily, why should I do it especially in Lent? Very true—Let us see, then, by your altered life and conduct that you have repented during this Lent, and then it will be time to talk of repenting every day after Lent. But, in fact, a man might just as well argue, I say my prayers every day, and God hears them, why should I say them more on Sundays than any other day? Why? not only because your forefathers, and the Church of your forefathers, have advised you, which, though not an imperative reason, is still a strong one, surely, but because the thing is good, and reasonable, and right in itself. Because, as they found in their own case, and as you may find in yours, if you will but think, the hurry and bustle of business is daily putting repentance and self-examination out of our heads. A man may think much, and pray much, thank God, in the very midst of his busiest work, but he is apt to be hurried; he has not set his thoughts especially on the matters of his soul, and so the soul's work is not thoroughly done. Much for which he ought to pray he forgets to pray for. Many sins and feelings of which he ought to repent slip past him out of sight in the hurry of life. Much good that might be done is put off and laid by, often till it is too late. But now here is a regular season in which we may look back and say to ourselves, 'How have I been getting on for this twelvemonth, not in pocket, but in character? not in the appearance of character in my neighbour's eyes, but in real character—in the eyes of God? Am I more manly, or more womanly—more godly, more true, more humble, above all, more loving, than I was this time last year? What bad habits have I conquered? What good habits have grown upon me? What chances of doing good have I let slip? What foolish, unkind things have I done? My duty to God and my neighbours is so and so, how have I done it? Above all, this Saviour and King in heaven, in whom I profess to believe, to whom I have sworn to be loyal and true, and to help His good cause, the cause of godliness, manliness, and happiness among my neighbours, in my family, in my own heart,—how have I felt towards Him? Have I thought about Him more this year than I did last? Do I feel any more loyalty, respect, love, gratitude to Him than I did? Ay, more, do I think about Him at all as a living man, much less as my King and Saviour; or, is all really know about Him the sound of the words Jesus Christ, and the story about Him in the Apostles' Creed? Do I really *believe* and trust in "Jesus Christ," or do I not? These are sharp, searching questions, my friends,—good Lenten food for any man's soul,—questions which it is much more easy to ask soberly and answer fairly now when you look quietly back on the past year, than it is, alas! to answer them day by day amid all the bustle your business and your families. But you will answer, 'This bustle will go on just as much in Lent as ever. Our time and thoughts will be just as much occupied. We have our livings to get. We are not fine gentlemen and ladies who can lie by for forty days and do nothing but read and pray, while their tradesmen and servants are working for them from morning to night. How then can we give up more time to religion now than at other times?

This is all true enough; but there is a sound and true answer to it. It is not so much more *time* which you are asked to give up to your souls in Lent, as it is more *heart*. What do I talk of? *Giving up* more time to your souls? And yet this is the way we all talk, as if our time belonged to our bodies, and so we had to rob them of it, to give it up to our souls,—as if our bodies were ourselves, and our souls were troublesome burdens, or peevish children hanging at our backs, which would keep prating and fretting about heaven and hell, and had to be quieted, and their mouths stopped as quickly and easily as possible, that we might be rid of them, and get about our true business, our real duty,—this mighty work of eating and drinking, and amusing ourselves, and making money. I am afraid—afraid there are too many, who, if they spoke out their whole hearts, would be quite as content to have no souls, and no necessity to waste their precious time (as they think) upon religion. But, my friends, my friends, the day will come when you will see yourselves in a true light; when your soul will not seem a mere hanger-on to your body, but you will find out *that you are your soul*. Then there will be no more forgetting that you have souls, and thrusting them into the background, to be fed at odd minutes, or left to starve,—no more talk of *giving up* time to the care of your souls; your souls will take the time for themselves then—and the eternity, too; they will be all in all to you then, perhaps when it is too late!

Well, I want you, just for forty days, to let your souls be all in all to you now; to make them your first object—your first thought in the morning, the last thing at night,—your thought at every odd moment in the day. You need not neglect your business; only for one short forty days do not make your business your God. We are all too apt to try the heathen plan, of seeking first every thing else in the world, and letting the kingdom of God and His righteousness be added to us over and above—or *not* as it may happen. Try for once the plan the Lord of heaven and earth advises, and seek first the kingdom of God and His righteousness, and see whether every thing else will not be added to you. Again, you need not be idle a moment more in Lent than at any other time. But I dare say, that none of you are so full of business that you have not a free ten minutes in the morning, and ten minutes at night, of which the best of uses may be made. What do I say? Why, of all men in the world, farmers and labourers have most time, I think, to themselves; working, as they do, the greater part of their day in silence and alone; what opportunities for them to have their souls busy in heaven, while they are pacing over the fields, ploughing and hoeing! I have read of many, many labouring men who had found out their opportunities in this way, and used them so well as to become holy, great, and learned men. One of the most learned scholars in England at this day was once a village carpenter, who used, when young, to keep a book open before him on his bench while he worked, and thus contrived to teach himself, one after the other, Latin, Greek, and Hebrew. So much time may a man find who *looks* for time!

But after all, and above all, believe this—that if your business or your work does actually give you no time to think about God and your own souls,—if in the midst of it all you cannot find leisure enough night and morning to pray earnestly, to read your Bible carefully,—if it so swallows up your whole thoughts during the day, that you have no opportunity to recollect yourself, to remember that you are an immortal being, and that you have a Saviour in heaven, whom you are serving faithfully, or unfaithfully,—if this work or business of yours will not give you time enough for that, then it is not God's business, and ought not to be yours either.

But you have time,—you have all time. When there is a will there is a way. Make up your minds that there shall be a will, and pray earnestly to God to give it you, if it is but for forty days: and in them think seriously, slowly, solemnly, over your past lives. Examine yourselves and your doings. Ask yourselves fairly,—'Am I going forward or back? Am I living like a child of God, or like a mere machine for making food and wages? Is my conduct such as the Holy Scripture tells me that it should be? You will not need to go far for a set of questions, my friends, or rules by which to examine yourselves. You can hardly open a page of God's blessed Book without finding something which stares you in the face with the question,

'Do I do thus?' or, 'Do I not do thus?' Take, for example, the Epistle of this very day. What better test can we have for trying and weighing our own souls?

What says it? That though we were wise, charitable, eloquent—all that the greatest of men can be, and yet had not charity—*love*, we are nothing!—nothing! And how does it describe this necessary, indispensable, heavenly love? Let us spend the last few minutes of this sermon in seeing how. And if that description does not prick all our hearts on more points than one, they are harder than I take them for—far harder, certainly, than they should be.

This charity, or love, we hear, which each of us ought to have and must have—"suffers long, and is kind." What shall we say to that? How many hasty, revengeful thoughts and feelings have risen in the hearts of most of us in the last year?—Here is one thought for Lent. "Charity envies not."—Have we envied any their riches, their happiness, their good name, health, and youth?—Another thought for Lent. "Charity boasts not herself." Alas! alas! my friends, are not the best of us apt to make much of the little good we do,—to pride ourselves on the petty kindnesses we shew,—to be puffed up with easy self-satisfaction, just as charity is *not* puffed up?—Another Lenten thought. "Charity does not behave herself unseemly;" is never proud, noisy, conceited; gives every man's opinion a fair, kindly hearing; making allowances for all mistakes. Have we done so?—Then there is another thought for Lent. "Charity seeks not her own;" does not stand fiercely and stiffly on her own rights, on the gratitude due to her. While we—are we not too apt, when we have done a kindness, to fret and fume, and think ourselves deeply injured, if we do not get repaid at once with all the humble gratitude we expected? Of this also we must think. "Charity thinks no evil," sets down no bad motives for any one's conduct, but takes for granted that he means well, whatever appearances may be; while we (I speak of myself just as much as of any one), are we not continually apt to be suspicious, jealous, to take for granted that people mean harm; and even when we find ourselves mistaken, and that we have cried out before we are hurt, not to consider it as any sin against our neighbour, whom in reality we have been silently slandering to ourselves? "Charity rejoices not in iniquity," but in the truth, whatever it may be; is never glad to see a high professor prove a hypocrite, and fall into sin, and shew himself in his true foul colours; which we, alas! are too apt to think a very pleasant sight.—Are not these wholesome meditations for Lent? "Charity hopes all things" of every one, "believes all things," all good that is told of every one, "endures all things," instead of flying off and giving up a person at the first fault. Are not all these points, which our own hearts, consciences, common sense, or whatever you like to call it (I shall call it God's spirit), tell us are right, true, necessary? And is there one of us who can say that he has not offended in many, if not in all these points; and is not that unrighteousness—going out of the right, straightforward, childlike, loving way of looking at all people? And is not all unrighteousness sin? And must not all sin be repented of, and that *as soon as we find it out?* And can we not all find time this Lent to throw over these sins of ours?—to confess them with shame and sorrow?—to try like men to shake them off? Oh, my friends! you who are too busy for forty short days to make your immortal souls your first business, take care—take care, lest the day shall come when sickness, and pain, and the terror of death, shall keep you too busy to prepare those unrepenting, unforgiven, sin-besotted souls of yours for the kingdom of God.

SERMON XXIV.
ON BOOKS.

JOHN, i. 1.

"In the beginning was the Word, and the Word was with God, and the Word was God."

I DO not pretend to be able to explain this text to you, for no man can comprehend it but He of whom it speaks, Jesus Christ, the Word of God. But I can, by God's grace, put before you some of the awful and glorious truths of which it gives us a sight, and may Christ direct you, who is *the* Word, and grant me words to bring the matter home to you, so as to make some of you, at least, ask yourselves the golden question, 'If this is true, what must we *do* to be saved?'

The text says that the Word was from the beginning with God,—ay, God Himself: who the Word is, there is no doubt from the rest of the chapter, which you heard read this morning. But why is Christ called the Word of all words—the Word of God? Let us look at this. Is not Christ *the man*, the head and pattern of all men who are what men ought to be? And did He not tell men that He is *the* Life? That all life is given by Him and out of Him? And does not St. John tell us that Christ the Life is the light of men,—the true light which lighteth every man who cometh into the world?

Remember this, and then think again,—what is it which makes men different from all other living things we know of? Is it not speech—the power of words? The beasts may make each other understand many things, but they have no speech. These glorious things—words—are man's right alone, part of the image of the Son of God—the Word of God, in which man was created. If men would but think what a noble thing it is merely to be able to speak in words, to think in words, to write in words! Without words, we should know no more of each other's hearts and thoughts than the dog knows of his fellow dog;—without words to think in; for if you will consider, you always think to yourself in *words*, though you do not speak them aloud; and without them all our thoughts would be mere blind longings, feelings which we could not understand our own selves. Without words to write in, we could not know what our forefathers did;—we could not let our children after us know what to do. But, now, books—the written word of man—are precious heirlooms from one generation to another, training us, encouraging us, teaching us, by the words and thoughts of men, whose bodies are crumbled into dust ages ago, but whose words—the power of uttering themselves, which they got from the Son of God—still live, and bear fruit in our hearts, and in the hearts of our children after us, till the last day!

But where did these words—this power of uttering our thoughts, come from? Do you fancy that men first, began like brute beasts or babies, with strange cries and mutterings, and so gradually found out words for themselves? Not they; the beasts have been on the earth as long as man; and yet they can no more speak than they could when God created Adam: but Adam, we find, could speak at once. God spoke to Adam the moment he was made, and Adam understood Him; so he knew the power and the meaning of words. Who gave him that power? Who but Jehovah—Jesus—the Word of God, who imparted to him the word of speech and the light of reason? Without them what use would there have been in saying to him, "Thou shalt not eat of the tree of knowledge?" Without them what would there have been in God's bringing to him all the animals to see what he would call them, unless He had first given Adam the power of understanding words, and thinking of words, and speaking words? This was the glorious gift of Christ—the Voice or Word of the Lord God, as we read in the second chapter of Genesis, whom Adam heard another time with fear and terror,—"The voice of the Lord walking in the garden in the cool of the day."—A text and a story strange enough, till we find in the first chapter of St. John the explanation of it, telling us that the Word was in the beginning with God—very God, and that He was the light which lighteth every man who cometh into the world. So Christ is the light which lighteth every man who cometh into the world. How are we to understand that, when there are so many who live and die heathens or reprobates,—some who never hear of Christ,—some, alas! in Christian lands, who are dead to every doctrine or motive of Christianity? yet the Bible says that Christ lights *every man* who comes into the world. Difficult to understand at first sight, yet most true, and simple too, at bottom.

For how is every one, whether heathen or Christian, child or man, enlightened or taught, to live and behave? Is it not by the words of those round him, by the words he reads in books, by the thoughts which he thinks out and puts into shape for himself? All this is the light which every human being has his share of. And has not every man, too, the light of reason and good feeling, more or less, to tell him whether each thing is right or wrong, noble or mean, ugly or beautiful? This is another way by which the light which lighteth every man works. And St. John tells us in the text, that he who works in this way,—he who gives us the power of understanding, and thinking, and judging, and speaking, is the very same Word of God who was made flesh, and dwelt among men, and died on the Cross for us; "the Lamb of God, who taketh away the sins of the world!"

He is the Word of God—by Him God has spoken to man in all ages. He taught Adam,—He spoke to Abraham as a man speaketh with his friend. It was He Jehovah, whom we call Jesus, whom Moses and the seventy elders saw—saw with their bodily eyes on Mount Sinai, who spoke to them with human voice from amid the lightning and the rainbow. It must have been only He, the Word, by whom God the Father utters Himself to man, for no man hath seen God at any time; only the Word, the only-begotten Son, who is in the bosom of the Father, He hath declared Him. And who put into the mouth of David those glorious Psalms—the songs in which all true men for three thousand years have found the very things they longed to speak themselves and could not? Who but Christ the Word of God, the Lord, as David calls Him, put a new song into the mouth of His holy poet,—the sweet singer of Israel? Who spake by the prophets, again? What do they say themselves?—"The Word of the Lord came to me, saying." And then, when the Spirit of God stirred them up, the Word of God gave them speech, and they said the sayings which shall never pass away till all be fulfilled. And who was it who, when He was upon earth, spake as never man spake,—whose words were the simplest, and yet the deepest,—the tenderest, and yet the most awful, which ever broke the blessed silence upon this earth,—whose words, now to this day, come home to men's hearts, stirring them up to the very roots, piercing through the marrow of men's souls,—whose but Christ's, the Word, who was made flesh and dwelt among us, full of grace and truth? And who since then, do you think, has it been who has given to all wise and holy poets, philosophers, and preachers, the power to speak and write the wonderful truths which, by God's grace, they thought out for themselves and for all mankind,—who gave them utterance?—who but Christ, the Lord of men's spirits, the Word of God, who promised to give to all His true disciples a mouth and wisdom, which their enemies should not be able to gainsay or resist?

Well, my friends, ought not the knowledge of this to make us better and wiser? Ought it not to make us esteem, and reverence, and use many things of which we are apt to think too lightly? How it should make us reverence the Bible, the written word of God's saints and prophets, of God's apostles, of Christ, the Word Himself? Oh, that men would use that treasure of the Bible as it deserves;—oh, that they would believe from their hearts, that whatever is said there is truly said, that whatever is said there is said to them, that whatever names things are called there are called by their right names. Then men would no longer call the vile person beautiful, or call pride and vanity honour, or covetousness respectability, or call sin worldly wisdom; but they would call things as Christ calls them—they would try to copy Christ's thoughts and Christ's teaching; and instead of looking for instruction and comfort to lying opinions and false worldly cunning, they would find their only advice in the blessed teaching, and their only comfort in the gracious promises, of the word of the Book of Life.

Again, how these thoughts ought to make us reverence all books. Consider! except a living man, there is nothing more wonderful than a book!—a message to us from the dead—from human souls whom we never saw, who lived, perhaps, thousands of miles away; and yet these, in those little sheets of paper, speak to us, amuse us, terrify us, teach us, comfort us, open their hearts to us as brothers.

Why is it that neither angels, nor saints, nor evil spirits, appear to men now to speak to them as they did of old? Why, but because we have *books*, by which Christ's messengers, and the devil's messengers too, can tell what they will to thousands of human beings at the same moment, year after year, all the world over! I say, we ought to reverence books, to look at them as awful and mighty things. If they are good and true, whether they are about religion or politics, farming, trade, or medicine, they are the message of Christ, the Maker of all things, the Teacher of all truth, which He has put into the heart of some man to speak, that he may tell us what is good for our spirits, for our bodies, and for our country.

And at the last day, be sure of it, we shall have to render an account—a strict account, of the books which we have read, and of the way in which we have obeyed what we read, just as if we had had so many prophets or angels sent to us.

If, on the other hand, books are false and wicked, we ought to fear them as evil spirits loose among us, as messages from the father of lies, who deceives the hearts of evil men, that they may spread abroad the poison of his false and foul messages, putting good for evil, and evil for good, sweet for bitter, and bitter for sweet, saying to all men, 'I, too, have a tree of knowledge, and you may eat of the fruit thereof, and not die.' But believe him not. When you see a wicked book, when you find in a book any thing which contradicts God's book, cast it away, trample it under foot, believe that it is the devil tempting you by his cunning, alluring words, as he tempted Eve, your mother. Would to God all here would make that rule,—never to look into an evil book, a filthy ballad, a nonsensical, frivolous story! Can a man take a snake into his bosom and not be bitten?—can we play with fire and not be burnt?—can we open our ears and eyes to the devil's message, whether of covetousness, or filth, or folly, and not be haunted afterwards by its wicked words, rising up in our thoughts like evil spirits, between us and our pure and noble duty—our baptism-vows?

I might say much more about these things, and, by God's help, in another sermon I will go on, and speak to you of the awful importance of spoken words, of the sermons and the conversation to which you listen, the awful importance of every word which comes out of your own mouth. But I have spoken only of books this morning, for this is the age of books, the time, one would think, of which Daniel prophesied that many should run to and fro, and knowledge should be increased. A flood of books, newspapers, writings of all sorts, good and bad, is spreading over the whole land, and young and old will read them. We cannot stop that—we ought not: it is God's ordinance. It is more: it is God's grace and mercy, that we have a free press in England—liberty for every man, that if he have any of God's truth to tell he may tell it out boldly, in books or otherwise. A blessing from God! one which we should reverence, for God knows it was dearly bought. Before our forefathers could buy it for us, many an honoured man left house and home to die in the battle-field or on the scaffold, fighting and witnessing for the right of every man to whom God's Word comes, to speak God's Word openly to his countrymen. A blessing, and an awful one! for the same gate which lets in good lets in evil. The law dare not silence bad books. It dare not root up the tares lest it root up the wheat also. The men who died to buy us liberty knew that it was better to let in a thousand bad books than shut out one good one; for a grain of God's truth will ever outweigh a ton of the devil's lies. We cannot then silence evil books, but we can turn away our eyes from them—we can take care that what we read, and what we let others read, shall be good and wholesome. Now, if ever, are we bound to remember that books are words, and that words come either from Christ or the devil,— now, if ever, we are bound to try all books by the Word of God,—now, if ever, are we bound to put holy and wise books, both religious and worldly, into the hands of all around us, that if, poor souls! they must need eat of the fruit of the tree of knowledge, they may also eat of the tree of life,—and now, if ever, are we bound to pray to Christ the Word of God, that He will raise up among us wise and holy writers, and give them words and utterance, to speak to the hearts of all Englishmen the message of God's covenant, and that he may confound the devil and his lies, and all that swarm of vile writers who are filling England with trash, filth, blasphemy, and covetousness, with books which teach men that our wise forefathers, who built our churches and founded our constitution, and made England the queen of nations, were but ignorant knaves and fanatics, and that selfish money-making and godless licentiousness are the only true wisdom; and so turn the divine power of words, and the inestimable blessing of a free press, into the devil's engine, and not Christ's the Word of God. But their words shall be brought to nought.

May God preserve us and all our friends from that defilement, and may He give you all grace, in these strange times, to take care what you read and how you read, and to hold fast by the Book of all books, and Christ the Word of God. Try by them all books and men; for if they speak not according to God's law and testimony, it is because there is no truth in them.

SERMON XXV.
THE COURAGE OF THE SAVIOUR.

JOHN, xi. 7, 8.

"Then after that saith He to His disciples, Let us go into Judea again. His disciples say to Him, Master, the Jews of late sought to stone thee, and goest thou thither again?"

WE all admire a brave man. And we are right. To be brave is God's gift. To be brave is to be like Jesus Christ. Cowardice is only the devil's likeness. But we must take care what we mean by being brave. Now, there are two sorts of bravery—courage and fortitude. And they are very different: courage is of the flesh,—fortitude is of the spirit. Courage is good, but dumb animals have it just as much as we. A dog, a tiger, and a horse, have courage, but they have no fortitude,—because fortitude is a spiritual thing, and beasts have no spirits like ours.

What is fortitude? It is the courage which will make us not only fight in a good cause, but suffer in a good cause. Courage will help us only to give others pain; fortitude will help us to bear pain ourselves. And more, fortitude will make a fearful person brave, and very often the more brave the more fearful they are. And thus it is that women are so often braver than men. We, men, are made of coarser stuff; we do not feel pain as keenly as women; and if we do feel, we are rightly ashamed to shew it. But a tender woman, who feels pain and sorrow infinitely more than we do, who need not be ashamed of being frightened, who perhaps is terrified at every mouse and spider,—to see her bearing patiently pain, and sorrow, and shame, in spite of all her fearfulness, because she knows it is her duty—that is Christ's likeness—that is true fortitude—that is a sight nobler than all the "bull-dog courage" in the world. For what is the courage of the bull-dog after all, or of the strong quarrelsome man? He is confident in his own strength, he is rough and hard, and does not care for pain; and when he thrusts his head into a fight, like a surly dog, he does it not because it is his duty, but because he likes it, because he is angry, and then every blow and every wound makes him more angry, and he fights on, forgetting his pain from blind rage.

That is not altogether bad; men ought to be courageous. But, oh! my friends, is there not a more excellent way to be brave? and which is nobler, to suffer bravely for God's sake, or to beat men made in God's image bravely for one's own sake? Think of any fight you ever saw, and then compare with that the stories of those old martyrs who died rather than speak a word against their Saviour. If you want to see true fortitude, think of what has happened thousands of times when the heathen used to persecute the Christians.— How delicate women, who would not venture to set the sole of their foot to the ground for tenderness, would submit, rather than give up their religion and deny the Lord who died for them, to be torn from husband and family, and endure nakedness, and insult, and tortures which make one's blood run cold to read of, till they were torn slowly piecemeal, or roasted in burning flames, without a murmur or an angry word,—knowing that Christ, who had borne all things for them, would give them strength to bear all things for Him, trusting that if they were faithful unto death, He would give them a crown of life. There was true fortitude—there was true faith—there was God's strength made perfect in woman's weakness! Do you not see, my friends, that such a death was truly brave? How does bull-dog courage shew beside that courage—the courage which conquers grief and pain for duty's-sake, instead of merely forgetting them in rage and obstinacy?

And do you not see how this bears on my text? How it bears on our Lord's whole life? Was he not indeed the perfectly brave man—the man who endured more than all living men put together, at the very time that he had the most intense fear of what he was going to suffer? And stranger still, endured it all of His own will, while He had it in His power to shake it all off any instant, and free Himself utterly from pain and suffering.

Now, this speech of our Lord's in the text is just a case of true fortitude. He was beyond Jordan. He had been forced to escape thither to save His life from the mad, blinded Jews. He had no foolhardiness; He knew that He had no more right than we have to put His life in danger when there was no good to be done by it. But now there *was* good to be done by it. Lazarus was dead, and He wanted to raise him to life. Therefore He said to His disciples, "Let us go into Judea again." They knew the danger; they said, "Master, the Jews of late sought to stone Thee, and goest Thou thither again?" But He would go; He had a work to do, and He dared bear anything to do His work. Ay, here is the secret, this is the feeling which gives a man true courage—the feeling that he has a work to do at all costs, the sense of duty. Oh! my friends, let men, women, or children, once feel that they have a duty to perform, let them once say to themselves, 'I am bound to do this thing—it is right for me to do this thing; I owe it as a duty to my family, I owe it as a duty to my country, I owe it as a duty to God, who called me into this station of life; I owe it as a duty to Jesus Christ, who bought me with His blood, that I might do His will and not my own pleasure.'—When a man has once said that *honestly* to himself, when that glorious heavenly thought, '*It is my duty,*' has risen upon his soul, like the sun upon the earth, warming his heart and enlightening it and making it bring forth all good and noble fruits, then that man will feel a strength come to him, and a courage from God above, which will conquer all his fears and his selfish love of ease and pleasure, and enable him to bear insults, and pain, and poverty, and death itself, provided he can but do what is right, and be found by God, whatever happens to him, working God's will where God has put him. This is fortitude—this is true courage—this is Christ's likeness—this is the courage which weak women on sick beds may have as well as strong men on the battle-field. Even when they shrink most from suffering, God's Spirit will whisper to them, 'It is *thy* duty, it is thy Father's will,' and then they will find His strength made perfect in their weakness, and when their human weakness fails most God will give them heavenly fortitude, and they will be able, like St. Paul, to say, "When I am weak, then I am strong, for I can do all things through Christ, who strengtheneth me."

And now, remember that there was no pride, no want of feeling to keep up our Lord's courage. He has tasted sorrow for every man, woman, and child, and therefore He has tasted fear also; tempted in all things, like as we are, that in all things He might be touched with the feeling of our infirmities,—that there might be no poor soul terrified at the thought of pain or sorrow, but could comfort themselves with the thought, Well, the Son of God knows what fear is. He who said that His soul was troubled—He who at the thought of death was in such agony of terror, that His sweat ran down to the ground like great drops of blood,—He who cried in His agony, "Father, if it be possible, let this cup pass from me,"—He understands my pain,—He tells me not to be ashamed of crying in my pain like Him, "Father, if it be possible let this cup pass from me"—for He will give me the strength to finish that prayer of His, and in the midst of my trouble say, "Nevertheless, Father, not as I will, but as Thou wilt." Remember, again, that our Lord was not like the martyrs of old, forced to undergo His sufferings whether He liked them or not. We are too apt to forget that, and therefore we misunderstand our Lord's example; and therefore we misunderstand what true fortitude is. Jesus Christ was the Son of God; He had made the very men who were tormenting Him; He had made the very wood of the cross on which He hung, the iron which pierced His blessed hands; and, for aught we know, one wish of His, and they would all have crumbled into dust, and He have been safe in a moment. But He would not; He *endured* the cross. He was the only man who ever really endured anything at all, because He alone of all men had perfect power to save Himself, even when He was nailed to the tree, fainting, bleeding, dying. It was never too late for Him to stop. As He said to Peter when he wanted to fight for Christ, "Thinkest thou that I cannot pray to my Father, and He will send me instantly more than twelve legions of angels?" But *He would not*. He had to save the world, and He was determined to do it, whatever agony or fear it cost Him. St. Peter was a *brave* man. He drew his sword in the garden, and attacked, single-handed, that great body of armed soldiers; cutting down a servant of the high-priest's. But he was only brave, our Lord was more. The blessed Jesus had true fortitude; He could *bear* patiently, while Peter could only rage and fight uselessly. And see how Christ's fortitude lasted Him, while Peter's mere courage failed him. While our Lord was witnessing that glorious confession of His before Pilate, bearing on through, without shrinking, even to the cross itself, where was Peter? He had denied his Master, and ran shamefully away. He had a long lesson to learn before he was perfect, had Peter. He had to learn not how to fight, but how to suffer—and he learnt it; and in his old age that strong, fierce St. Peter had true fortitude to give himself up to be crucified, like his Lord, without a murmur, and preach Christ's gospel as he hung for three whole days upon the torturing cross. There was fortitude; that violence of his in the garden was only courage as of a brute animal,—courage of the flesh, not the true courage of the spirit. Oh, my friends, that we could all learn this lesson, that it is better to suffer than to revenge, better to be killed than to kill. There are times when a man must fight—for his country, for just laws, for his family, but for himself it is very seldom that he must fight. He who returns good for evil,—he who when he is cursed, blesses those who curse him,—he, who takes joyfully the spoiling of his goods, who submits to be cheated in little matters, and sometimes in great ones, sooner than ruin the poor sinful wretch who has ill-used him; that man has really put on Christ's likeness, that man is really going on to perfection, and fulfilling the law of love; and for everything he gives up for the sake of peace and mercy, which is for God's sake, God will reward him sevenfold into his bosom. There are times when a man is bound to go to law, bound to expose and punish evil-doers, lest they should, being unpunished, become confident and go on from bad to worse, and hurt others as well as him. A man sometimes is bound by his duty to his neighbours and to society to defend himself, to go to law with those who injure him,—sometimes; but never bound to revenge himself, never bound to say, 'He has hurt me, and I will pay him off for it at law;' that is abusing law, which is God's ordinance, for mere selfish revenge. You may say, it is difficult to know which is which, when to defend oneself, and when not. It is difficult; without the light of God's Spirit, I think no man will know. But let a man live by God's Spirit, let him pray for kindliness, mercifulness, manliness, and patience, for true fortitude to bear and to forbear, and God will surely open his eyes to see when he is called on to avenge an injury, and when he is called on to suffer patiently. God will shew him—if a man wishes to be like Christ, and to work like Christ, at doing good, God will teach him and guide him in all puzzling matters like this. And do not be afraid of being called cowards and milksops for bearing injuries patiently—those who call you so will be likely to be the greatest cowards themselves. Patience is the truest sign of courage. Ask old soldiers, who have seen real war, and they will tell you that the bravest men, the men who endured best, not in mere fighting, but in standing still for hours to be mowed down by cannon-shot; who were most cheerful and patient in shipwreck, and starvation and defeat,—all things ten times worse than fighting,—ask old soldiers, I say, and they will tell you that the men who shewed best in such miseries, were generally the stillest and meekest men in the whole regiment: that is true fortitude; that is Christ's image—the meekest of men, and the bravest too. And so books say, and seem to prove it, by many strange stories, that the lion, while he is the strongest and bravest of beasts of prey, is also the most patient and merciful. He knows his own strength and courage, and therefore he does not care to be shewing it off. He can afford to endure an affront. It is only the cowardly cur who flies out and barks at every passer-by. And so with our blessed Lord. The Bible calls Him the Lion of Judah; but it also calls Him the Lamb dumb before the shearers. Ah, my friends, we must come back to Him, for all the little that is great and noble in man or woman, or dumb beast even, is perfected in Him; He only is perfectly great, perfectly noble, brave, meek. He who to save us sinful men, endured the cross, despising the shame, till He sat down at the right hand of the Majesty on high, perfectly brave He is, and perfectly gentle, and will be so for ever; for even at His second coming, when He shall appear the Conqueror of hell, with tens of thousands of angels, to take vengeance on those who know not God, and destroy the wicked with the breath of His mouth, even then in His fiercest anger, the Scripture tells us, His anger shall be "the anger of the Lamb." Almighty vengeance and just anger, and yet perfect gentleness and love all the while.—Mystery of mysteries!—The wrath of the Lamb! May God give us all to feel in that day, not the wrath, but the love of the Lamb who was slain for us!

FOOTNOTES

[92] "And when He was come to the other side, into the country of the Gergesenes, there met Him two possessed with devils, coming out of the tombs, exceeding fierce, so that no man might pass by that way. And, behold, they cried out, saying, What have we do with Thee, Jesus, Thou Son of God? Art Thou come hither to torment us before the time? And there was a good way off from them an herd of many swine feeding. So the devils besought him, saying, If Thou cast us out, suffer us to go away into the herd of swine. And He said unto them, Go. And when they were come out, they went into the herd of swine: and, behold, the whole herd of swine ran violently down a steep place into the sea, and perished in the waters."

[187] Von Stolberg.